THE ULTIMATE GUIDE TO
CATS

THE ULTIMATE GUIDE TO
CATS

Candida Frith-Macdonald

PaRragon

Bath · New York · Singapore · Hong Kong · Cologne · Delhi · Melbourne

First published by Parragon in 2009

Parragon
Queen Street House
4 Queen Street
Bath BA1 1HE, UK

Created and produced by

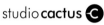

13 SOUTHGATE STREET WINCHESTER HAMPSHIRE SO23 9DZ

DESIGN Sharon Rudd
EDITORIAL Jennifer Close

ISBN: 978-1-4075-5528-7

Printed in China

STUDIO CACTUS WOULD LIKE TO THANK
Sharon Cluett for original styling; Jo Weeks for proofreading;
and Penelope Kent for indexing

PICTURE CREDITS
All images © Marc Henrie, ASC, except:
Animal Photography 42 bl; Chanan Photography/Richard
Katris 31 b, 59 br; Getty Images 11 c below r; Jim Brown
Photography 89 br; Jo-Anne Simpson 86 bl; Meryleen
Greenwood 25 b; NHPA 6 l, 13 tr, 24 bl, 33 b, 40 bl, 41, 50 br, 77
tr, 77 bl, 82 bl, 91 b, 92-93 tr, 92 bl; Photos.com 11 c above c,
11 c below c; Kristof Degreef 2–3; Shawn Hine 4 l; Mostakov
Roman 8 tr; Gunta Klavina 8 bl; Olga Utlyakova 9 bl; Vasiliy
Koval 9 br; Eric Isselée 10 bl; Tiberius Dinu 11 tl; Eric Isselée 11
tc; Dwight Smith 11 c above l; Jean Schweitzer 11 c above r;
Bochkarev Photography 11 c below l, 11 br; Gleb Semenjuk 12
cr; Magdalena Szachowska 13 c above r; Joshua Haviv 13 bl;
Claudia Carlsen 14 l; Eric Isselée 20 tl, 21 tl; Indigo Fish 64 tl;
Ekaterina Cherkashina 93 br; Diane Webb 94 l.

COVER IMAGES: Main Image: Somali Cat © Yann Arthus-
Bertrand / Corbis. Right hand side/back image: Red couch ©
Getty Images. Bottom left to right: European Burmese ©
NHPA; Abyssinian © Magdalena Szachowska; Siberian © akva

CONTENTS

ABOUT THIS BOOK

The cat has lived alongside us for several thousand years. In all that time, it has probably never changed so much or so rapidly as it has in the last hundred years. Of course, the basic feline physique, habits, and instincts remain much as they have been since the days of ancient Egypt, but our view of the cat, how we treat it and breed it, have changed radically.

THE FELINE PAST
Thanks to DNA analysis, we have a better idea than ever of where the domestic cat fits into the feline family, and when and where the most sociable and adventurous of wildcats began to hunt agricultural pests until a new type of cat, able to live in colonies and alongside another species, emerged. This change was largely psychological: Even when domesticated, the cat brought its magnificent senses and abilities into our homes intact.

THE FELINE PRESENT
After centuries in which it has been revered and protected, reviled and persecuted, and immortalized in pictures and prose, the cat has conquered every continent. Today, there are many cats that still come and go as they please and live partly on handouts, partly by their own skills, but the way we keep our cats has changed. Most now live into their late teens, due to vastly improved healthcare. But when the cat overtook the dog in popularity, many owners still really wanted a doglike pet, so there is a growing tendency to treat cats like dogs, and behavioral problems are on the rise.

THE FELINE FUTURE?
As the cat's popularity has risen, the kind of cat we own has become more important to some people. In most countries, pedigree cats are a tiny percentage of all pet cats, but in some places, primarily North America, they make up a substantial proportion of all cats owned. Here, the amateur world of the cat fancy is beginning to look highly professional, and attracting ever more controversy through breeds with curly ears, short legs, and wild feline blood. When the first GM cat appears, the fur will really fly.

SYMBOLS IN THIS BOOK

Symbols in the breed profiles give a quick reference guide. Build is not always apparent under an abundant coat; types are explained on pages 12–13. In temperament, cats generally vary between self-contained and dignified to chatty, "look at me" types; this is often classed as a Western/Oriental split, but breed origins are not always a guide. Coat care depends on more than coat length: The hairless breeds need more care than many longhairs. The swatches on profiles show a representative spread of popular colors.

BUILD			
	LEAN	MEDIUM	COBBY
TEMPERAMENT	PLACID	ACTIVE	
COAT CARE	LITTLE BRUSHING	BRUSH COAT TWICE A WEEK	BRUSH COAT DAILY

COAT COLORS

 BLACK SELF

 WHITE

 BLUE SELF

 BLUE SELF (LONG)

RED SELF

LILAC SELF

  BLACK & WHITE BLUE & WHITE RED & WHITE

BROWN CLASSIC TABBY

BROWN STRIPED TABBY

RED STRIPED TABBY

CREAM STRIPED TABBY

SILVER TABBY

SILVER STRIPED TABBY

LILAC STRIPED TABBY

BLUE SILVER TABBY

 BROWN TICKED TABBY (LONG)

 BLUE TICKED TABBY

RED TICKED TABBY

BROWN TICKED TABBY

 BLACK SMOKE

CHINCHILLA

SILVER SHADED

 TORTIE

 TORTIE & WHITE

TORTIE TABBY

TORTIE TABBY & WHITE

BLUE TABBY & WHITE

RED STRIPED TABBY & WHITE

BROWN TABBY & WHITE

    BLUE TORTIE & WHITE

BLUE TORTIE TABBY & WHITE

LILAC CREAM TORTIE

SEAL POINT

BLUE POINT

RED POINT

LILAC POINT

CARAMEL POINT

CREAM POINT

CHOCOLATE POINT

 FAWN POINT

 SEAL TABBY POINT

BLUE TABBY POINT

RED TABBY POINT & WHITE

LILAC TABBY POINT

HAIRLESS BREED COLORS

  BLACK SELF

LILAC SELF

BLACK & WHITE

 TORTIE

 TORTIE & WHITE

 BLUE TORTIE & WHITE

 SEAL POINT

BLUE POINT

COAT COLORS

All cats are tabbies in their genes, although they may have other genetic traits that cover up or suppress their pattern. The stripes of the tabby pattern are made up of areas of solid hairs set against areas of banded hairs produced by changes in pigment production. The main gene that controls whether a cat looks tabby or not is the agouti gene or allele. The dominant form (*A–*) shows the tabby pattern, but the recessive (*aa*) gives solid coats.

SOLID COLORS

Cats' coats are colored by melanin. This is made up of eumelanin (black and brown), and pheomelanin (red and yellow). Coat colors are produced by genes modifying these two. Solid color or melanism is caused by a recessive version of the tabby or agouti gene. Because two copies of the recessive form are needed (*aa*), melanism is uncommon.

The browning gene affects eumelanin and has three forms that give black (*B–*), chocolate (*bb*), and cinnamon (*blbl*). It can be modified by the dense pigment gene, which gives dense color in its dominant form (*D–*); the

WHITE Reduced melanocytes mean many white cats have blue eyes. As melanocytes in the inner ear are vital for passing sound to the brain, the white or spotting gene can cause deafness.

recessive form (*dd*) "dilutes" black to blue, chocolate to lilac, and cinnamon to fawn.

The orange gene in its recessive form (*o*) lets eumelanistic colors through. In its dominant form (*O*), it gives pheomelanistic red; dense and dilute modifier genes produce cream and apricot. *O* also suppresses the *aa* trait, letting tabby markings show. This gene is sex-linked, because it is located on the X chromosome. Males have only one X chromosome, so are either *O* or *o*. Because females have two X chromosomes, they can have red shades (*OO*), eumelanistic shades (*oo*), or tortoiseshell (*Oo*), a mix of red and black.

TABBY SHADES

The basic tabby pattern of the African wildcat is striped. This is called "mackerel" in the domestic cat, and is still the most common tabby pattern. Much later a new pattern appeared: The blotched or classic tabby. In this, the plain and agouti areas produce a swirling pattern. This is a recessive mutation of the striped tabby gene, and it remains less frequent in random breeds. The lines of both patterns may be broken up into spots, probably by a separate gene, known as the spotted tabby modifier.

Ticked tabbies, controlled by a ticked gene, have no solid colored hairs on the body at all: Every hair is banded with lighter agouti and darker areas. If just one copy of the ticked gene is present, it masks all other patterns.

SOLID COLORS The solid black or self coat was one of the first mutations to occur after the cat was domesticated, being recorded in Ancient Greece.

SMOKE, SHADED, AND TIPPED COLORS

The inhibitor gene is responsible for smokes, silver tabbies, and shaded or tipped coats. In its dominant form (*I–*), it causes hairs to be colored at the tip, and white at the base or all the way up the shaft. Smokes are always solid colors, meaning they have the recessive nonagouti (*aa*) pair or allele. Combined with the dominant inhibitor gene (*I–*), this gives a solid coat with a white undercoat. Silver tabbies have a clear tabby pattern, but the lighter areas are a clear silver-white, instead of the usual warmer shade. Shaded and tipped (often called "chinchilla") cats both have a silver undercoat with a soft overlay of their color in shaded cats, or a sparkling sprinkle of color on the very tips in a tipped cat. Both of these types, the patterned and the plain, are genetically some form of tabby pattern combined with the dominant inhibitor (*I–*) allele.

POINTED PATTERNS

Pointing is a form of partial, heat sensitive albinism, controlled by several mutations of the same gene, called *C*. This gene controls the first step in the production of pigment, causing it to be heat sensitive; pigment is only produced in the skin over cooler areas. This gives the characteristic darker "pointing" on the coolest parts of the body: The extremities of the legs and tail, and the face, which is cooled by air in the sinus cavities of the skull. Pointing will overlay all other possible patterns, so the extremities may be solid, tabby, or even silvered.

WHITE AND BICOLORED CATS

White in cats hides other colors beneath it. The other genes for color and pattern are still present in the cat, and will appear in any offspring. A white cat can be the result of three different genetic traits acting on melanocytes, the cells that make melanin. Firstly, it may be albino. Albinism disables melanocytes, resulting in a white coat and pink or blue-gray eyes.

The other two whites are an allover white gene and a white spotting gene. Both block the movement of the melanocytes in the embryo to the skin. This overrides all other genes for pigmentation to produce a white coat. Allover white caused by the dominant white gene *W* is often referred to as dominant white or epistatic white. Bicolors or white spotted cats are created by the dominant spotting gene *S*; a cat that carries two copies of this has more white than a cat with only one.

TABBY The word tabby appears around 1638, describing a fabric from Baghdad. By 1695, it was used for tabby cats, whose markings resembled this fabric.

SMOKE A silver undercoat beneath a solid self top coat, like this black smoke Persian, can be dramatic in cats with long or rexed coats, and shows especially well in movement.

POINTED This seal point is the classic Siamese shade. The color is genetically black, degraded to a very deep brown on the points and faded out to fawn or even cream over the body.

EYE COLORS

The colors of cats' eyes are extraordinary. Nothing like this range exists in the wild, or indeed in any other domestic animal. Dogs look up at us with big brown eyes, but a cat may look at a king with eyes of any shade from palest blue to softest green, or even deep, startling copper. The fanciful owner can even find a cat with eyes to match their own. But just what makes this rainbow of colors, and why are there so many?

WHAT MAKES UP EYE COLOR?

The first factor influencing eye color is the pigment in the iris. This is melanin, and gives shades from yellow through copper to brown or black. The other factor is the tissues over the iris. These are clear, because the cat needs to see through them, but just as glass has a tint when looked at edge on, this layer refracts light and influences the color, effectively giving a blue "tint."

These factors are not related, but vary separately. Together, they give a range of shades: Pale golden eyes come from light melanin and little tint, copper eyes from dark melanin and little tint, while pale green is the result of pale melanin and a deep tint, and deep green eyes of deep melanin and deep tint.

Neither factor is controlled by just one gene. Eye color is "polygenetic," which provides an infinite variety of subtle shades. Regardless of what breed standards call for, coat color and eye color are not genetically related: Blues can have copper eyes in the Burmese, and green in the Korat.

WHAT ABOUT BLUE EYES?

All kittens are born with blue eyes, and begin to develop their adult color after a few weeks. The exceptions are blue eyes found in pointed or white cats. In these cats, the iris is a pale pink because it has little or no melanin, and the eye color is determined by the refraction of light alone. The eyes are pale blue in most Western cats, but deep blue in Siamese. There are also some Orientals that have fully colored bodies but eyes tantalizingly close to blue. Just how this trait is produced and passed on could prove interesting.

WILD EYES Just as the default coat of the cat is a brown tabby, the default eye color is hazel. This sits roughly in the middle of the spectrum of colors seen in breeds.

PALE GOLD With no blue and the palest yellow iris, this color is common in random breeds and found in some breeds that emphasize a natural look, such as the Norwegian Forest Cat.

MID GOLD This deeper, more striking tint is preferred in many breeds, for example in the Bombay, an American breed that was created to resemble a black panther.

DEEP COPPER This is the classic eye color associated with most colors of Persian. It shows up well against the coats of blue breeds, such as the Chartreux.

PALE GREEN This blend of pale gold and a light blue tint is a classic shade with a black coat in random breeds. It is essential for breeds such as the Korat.

MID GREEN This deeper shade is created by a strong blue tint, and so it is associated slightly more with Eastern cats than European types. It is found in the Oriental breeds.

DEEP GREEN This shade looks particularly striking with silver coats, and is often aspired to in silver tabbies. In shaded and tipped silver coats, an even bluer shade is sometimes called for.

PALE BLUE This china blue is generally associated with white or bicolor cats, but pale shades are also found in some pointed cats if they have not been bred selectively for a deep blue.

MID BLUE Deeper blues are found mainly in pointed cats. In related breeds, a very pale underlying iris may occasionally give a shade that is almost blue in a nonpointed cat.

DEEP BLUE This is the epitome of the Siamese, and now exported into other breeds. Although the early cats had quite light eyes, breeders now reliably get deep blues.

HUMAN INFLUENCE

African wildcat eyes are hazel-gold, with only a faint hint of green. Even in domestic cats, the most common eye colors are in the middle of the possible ranges: Gold to a golden-green. These are produced by moderate amounts of melanin and a moderate blue tint. The deeper tones produced by more melanin are less commonly seen, and these are the colors that pedigree breeders pursue.

Breeders have also pursued deep blue eyes in Siamese; the eyes of the breed today are darker than those seen in the ordinary pointed cats of Thailand, which can have eyes as light as a white cat. This deeper cast extends to the other Oriental breeds, whose green eyes tend to be deeper and bluer than the green eyes of Western breeds. When the Siamese has been crossed with other breeds to introduce the colorpoint pattern, the intensity has usually been diminished.

DIFFERENT GENE, SAME COLOR People sometimes assume that the blue eyes of pointed cats are by their nature always darker than those of white cats. This is not so; some pointed cats have simply been bred for darker eyes.

BUILD AND SHAPE

Shape or "type" is a major part of what defines a breed. The length and thickness of the legs, and the relative sturdiness or slenderness of the body, are essential to the overall picture. Just as feline build varies from svelte to sturdy, so the shape of the head and set of its features vary from one breed to another. In addition, within a breed, fashions, and so breed standards, vary from place to place and from one era to another.

BUILD

"Cold climate cats" have a sturdy, heat-conserving build, known as cobby. A good example is the Persian or the Exotic. The ideal is a short, wide body with a deep chest, carried relatively low on short, thick legs that end in large, round paws. Even the tail is relatively short and thick. The massiveness of the body should be the result of heavy boning and muscle. A slightly less massive build is classed as semicobby. Exactly where "cobby" shades into "semicobby" is tricky to define, and varies with the breed association or country.

Breeds of medium body conformation sit somewhere in the middle of the range. Their bodies are neither short and broad nor long and slender, but are a well-proportioned rectangle. Their boning is neither heavy nor fine, their legs slender but not model thin, and should not look markedly long in relation to the body. The overall look might best be described as athletic. One example is the Abyssinian.

Foreign and semiforeign builds are associated with breeds from the Orient, although some of the modern breeds created in the West will have this build. The semiforeign body is lithe and slender. The graceful legs look long in relation to the body. Breeds of semiforeign type include the Russian, the Tonkinese, or the Egyptian Mau. Foreign cats are altogether more svelte. These are "warm climate" looks, with everything geared to maximum surface area for the size, allowing a cat to keep cool. The body is long and tubular, the legs long and slender, the tail long and thin. This is the look of the Siamese, and the Oriental Shorthair and Longhair.

COBBY CAT The Exotic has no long coat to hide any possible deficiencies in build and make it look rounder than it is.

COBBY OR SEMICOBBY The British Shorthair is described both ways. Its build is strong, but should never be portly or thuggish.

FOREIGN The Oriental Shorthair is typical of the look expected in Far Eastern breeds. The emphasis here is on a delicate structure rarely, if ever, seen in free-breeding cats, even in Southeast Asia.

SEMIFOREIGN The Russian Shorthairs are of a lean but muscular type, with legs that are longer in relation to the body than in more European types, but still strong and sturdy-looking.

HEAD SHAPE

To complement their broad bodies, cobby breeds have broad, rounded heads with full cheeks and wide muzzles. This is the look of many old Western breeds, like the American Shorthair. The profile usually shows a "break" or change of angle between the eyes, leading down into a short, broad nose and muzzle with a strong chin. The eyes are generally large, with a shape ranging from round to a broad oval, level, and widely spaced. In general, the ears are short, broad at the base, and rounded at the tips. They tend to be fairly upright at the corners of the head.

Breeds with faces described as "modified wedges" with curves fall into the category of medium heads. The forehead flows into the nose in a continuous curve rather than with a stop or break. The eyes are round to oval, but may be set at more of a slant than in cobby faces, and the ears tend to be larger than on cobby heads, but still broad rather than long, and rounded over the tips.

Less modified "modified wedges" shift into the foreign category, where the look is more angular; some call the less dramatic examples "semiforeign." The whole head is longer and narrower, and the planes range from shallow curves to near flat. The profile tends to be straighter, leading into a muzzle that is no longer rounded, but tapering. The eyes are distinctly oval and set on a slant, and inevitably closer together, while the ears are large, long, and pointed at the tips. This is the look of breeds from the Russian Shorthair to the Siamese.

COBBY HEAD Broad, strong, and rounded in every part, this is the classic cobby head. Due to the large muzzle and full whisker pads, cats with this face type often look as if they are smiling.

MEDIUM HEAD The expression of the Bengal is intense and singular, but the broad, medium wedge with gentle curves and slightly rounded chin holds back from extremes to give a good example of a moderate type.

FOREIGN HEAD This distinctively triangular face with large, flaring ears is typical of the Oriental Shorthair and all related breeds. The profile is no less distinctive, having a long, smooth line with only a slight dip at the eyes.

Changing looks

Cat types do not stand still over time. By and large, there has been a drift away from the middle ground towards the more striking, dramatic ends of the spectrum. Standards tend to be more exaggerated in North America than they are in Europe, with the cobby cats being more massive and the foreign cats more etiolated. The phrase "ultra type" is sometimes used of the more exaggerated examples of both. Health concerns about head shapes are part of the often heated controversy over so-called ultra types. At one extreme is the Persian, which originally had a longer, more recognizably feline nose. Gradually, it became shorter: The result is impaired breathing and blocked tear ducts. At the other extreme is the Siamese, with a narrow head and slanted eyes. Detractors complain that the "haw," usually hidden in the inner corner of the eye, is increasingly visible.

PERSIAN NOSE Red Persians were the source of the "Peke-face," no longer seen but echoed in the general type. The U.K. Governing Council of the Cat Fancy (GCCF) standard calls for the nose leather to be below the bottom of the eyes.

MUTATIONS Some breeds are defined by a mutation, such as the Manx. Its short or absent tail, results from a gene with damaging side effects.

BREED CATALOGUE

Most cat breeds are differentiated by the length and type of coat. The domestic cat's ancestor, the African wildcat, has a close-lying, short coat, and the cat that spread across Europe and to the Orient had this coat. Longhaired cats were brought to Europe from both Persia and Turkey in the 16th and 17th centuries, and it is generally thought the mutation for long hair arose there, but the trait may have appeared independently in several places: Some genes are "hotspots" for mutation. Curly (rexed) and even absent coats have cropped up throughout history, but have usually remained relatively local oddities and died out over time, because they are a significant disadvantage to a self-supporting cat. Other breeds are defined by unusual features, such as curled ears or truncated tails. And, finally, a new growth area is experimental hybrids between the domestic cat and wildcats, of which the Bengal is an early success story.

NORWEGIAN FOREST CAT This brown tabby shows the slightly wild look preferred in what is a natural breed. The lynx tipping and long furnishings in the ear are key, and tabby coats are highly popular.

EXOTIC

ORIGIN United States (1960s)

SYNONYM None

WEIGHT 8–15 lb. (3.5–7 kg.)

BUILD

TEMPERAMENT

COAT CARE

COLORS All colors in self, tortie, bicolor, smoke, shaded, and tipped; classic, striped, and spotted tabby patterns; pointed pattern

The Exotic is a teddy bear of a cat, with a soft, plush coat; a soft, slightly squeaky voice; and round, bright eyes in the middle of a round, foreshortened face. It is essentially a shorthaired Persian, with the same gentle, quiet personality but without the chore of daily brushing to keep it looking good.

BLACK SELF   BLUE SELF   BROWN CLASSIC TABBY   RED STRIPED TABBY   SILVER SHADED   LILAC POINT

BREED ORIGINS

The first Exotic breeders were aiming to introduce the silver coat and green eyes of the shaded or tipped chinchilla Persians into the American Shorthair when they made the first crosses between the breeds in the 1950s. The result was a handsome cat with the coat they wanted but a face and body that were far from the American Shorthair look. It was suggested in the 1960s that these crosses should be developed as a breed in themselves, and the name Exotic was coined. Several other breeds were used in the development of the Exotic, including the Burmese and even the Russian Shorthair.

The Exotic's breed standard originally differed from that of the Persian, and some Persian breeders feared that interbreeding of Exotics and Persians would produce Persians with inferior coats or longer faces. As the breed progressed in the 1970s, however, the standard was amended to bring it closer to that of the Persian. The breed standards for the Exotic now match those for the Persian in all but coat length: They call for a rounded cat with stocky legs, and a large, round head with a sweet expression. The breed has been fully recognized by every major registry.

OWNING AN EXOTIC

Although short enough not to matt or tangle, the coat is thicker and more "plush" than that of many other shorthair breeds. A little extra grooming once or twice a week will keep it glossy and soft. The face may need more frequent attention, due to some inherent problems of the "pansy-like" shortened look.

When it comes to behavior, owners often say that the Exotic is a more active and outgoing cat than its longhaired cousin. This may simply be a happy result of not being burdened by a heavy and insulating coat all year. In their basic character,

RED All red and cream cats show tabby markings, and one effect of the short coat of the Exotic is that markings show up more clearly than in a longhair.

Exotic popularity

Over the decades, the Exotic has been steadily creeping up in popularity. It has almost made it into the top ten most popular breeds in the United Kingdom, where it seems to be holding steady while the Persian declines, and it is the most popular shorthair breed and third most popular breed overall in the United States.

BROWN CLASSIC TABBY The blotched or classic tabby pattern shows well in a Persian coat. The Exotic's short coat shows off stripes and spots just as well, but the classic remains a classic.

TORTOISESHELL Blacks, reds, and the tortoiseshells that result from crossing these remain among the most popular colors for the Exotic breed.

however, Exotics are much the same as Persians. They are easygoing, self-contained, and quiet cats, affectionate without being noisily demanding.

The Exotic suffers from the same health concerns as the Persian. They have a similarly high incidence of the inherited disorder polycystic kidney disease (PKD), although DNA testing should help breeders to eliminate carriers from breeding programs. Because it shares the breed standard for a brachycephalic face with the Persian, the Exotic also shares the eye problems and breathing difficulties associated with the look.

British Shorthair

ORIGIN United Kingdom (1800s)

SYNONYM None

WEIGHT 9–18 lb. (4–8 kg.)

BUILD

TEMPERAMENT

COAT CARE

COLORS All colors in self, tortie, bicolor, smoke, and tipped; blotched, striped, and spotted tabby; pointed pattern

One of the very first breeds to be given a standard and actively bred, the British Shorthair is an elder statesman of the feline fancy. And this is about as masculine as a cat breed can get: Chunky and robust, it is a no-nonsense, cobby cat that scorns flashy features or fluffy coats.

BLUE SELF · RED SELF · BLACK & WHITE · CREAM STRIPED TABBY · SILVER STRIPED TABBY · SILVER SHADED

BREED ORIGINS

The ancestors of the British Shorthair were working cats, from farm cats to urban mousers. When deliberate breeding began, this was the natural starting stock. The founder of the cat fancy, Harrison Weir, bred British Shorthairs, and it was the most popular breed at early shows.

Two World Wars and the growing popularity of exotics had a devastating effect on breeding, and by 1950, the breed was almost extinct. Dedicated breeders in Britain and throughout the Commonwealth began working to bring it back from the brink, using outcrosses to Oriental Shorthairs and Persians to bolster the small gene pool. By the 1970s, it was back in business, and the breed was even becoming known in the United States. Today, the British Shorthair is once again top cat in its homeland. It toppled the Persian from the number one spot in 2001, and has stayed there ever since. It is also popular in the United States, where it holds its own just outside the top ten.

OWNING A BRIT

This breed is muscular, neither extremely cobby nor lean. The legs are short and strong; the rounded head is carried on a short, sturdy neck; and the coat is a dense, weatherproof plush that feels crisp rather than soft. The coat is easycare, needing no day-to-day maintenance and just a quick brush to bring out its luster.

RED TABBY POINT The pointed colors are still something of a novelty, with some breeders specializing in them.

SILVER TABBY Silvers were among the very first examples of the breed shown in the 1880s, and remain popular today.

BLACK SELF The combination of lustrous jet black coat with the copper eye color so rarely seen in non-pedigrees is one of the most popular types today.

In character, the British Shorthair is literally down to earth: These cats dislike being picked up and handled all the time. Perhaps fortunately, given their substantial weight and size, these are not dependent types that want constant attention, stroking, and to use you as a cushion.

These cats have the intelligence of a natural survivor, but not insatiable inquisitiveness. British Shorthairs are essentially sensible, reliable, perhaps rather stolid cats.

The stocky build of the British Shorthair does hint at one weakness: This is a breed inclined to obesity. Instead of free feeding, read the guidelines on the packaging of the food you buy and then stick to them.

BLUE SELF This, more than any other color, typifies the British Shorthair. It was among the first colors bred and shown in Victorian Britain, and it remains the most widely shown color today.

Chartreux

ORIGIN France (before 1700s)

SYNONYM None

WEIGHT 7–17 lb. (3–7.5 kg.)

BUILD 🐈

TEMPERAMENT 🐱

COAT CARE ✂️

COLORS Blue self only

This cloud-colored cat is the French Shorthair in everything but name. The Chartreux was named "cat of France" and *Felis catus coeruleus* by the 18th-century naturalist Buffon, and was the pet chosen by the French President General de Gaulle and championed by the flamboyant author Colette. Despite lapses in its fortunes during the 20th century, the breed survived to stage a comeback, and the "smiling cat" remains an icon of its homeland today.

CHARTREUX SHADES The coat may be any shade of blue from a pale ashy shade to a deep slate, although the brighter shades are preferred on the show bench in all the registries.

BREED ORIGINS

The origins of this breed are wrapped in legends. It has been claimed to be descended from cats that lived with Carthusian monks in the Chartreuse monastery, but there are no records of any such blue cats in the monastery archives. Another tale says that the ancestors of the Chartreux were brought to France from Syria in the 13th century by returning crusaders, many of whom became Carthusian monks. Stocky gray cats with copper eyes are referred to as "the cats of Syria" in 16th-century French sources. But it seems likely that the name in fact comes from a Spanish woolen fabric called "pile de Chartreux," just as the tabby pattern was named after a cloth. This hints at a darker past for these cats: They were prized by furriers for their luxuriant pelts.

Chartreux cats lived in small, natural colonies scattered across France, notably in Paris and on Belle Île, off the coast of Brittany. Two world wars were hard on the numbers, and outcrosses were made to other cats, based almost entirely on their color: Blue Persians, blue British Shorthairs and blue Russian Shorthairs. The breed was considered so close to the British in type that the European registry body, the Fédération Internationale Féline (FIFé), declared the two to be one in 1970: Concerted work and campaigning by breeders saw this reversed by 1977.

OWNING A CHARTREUX

The Chartreux coat is a soft plush of an even blue, with an overall silvery sheen, setting off eyes in shades from gold to deepest copper. The build has been called "primitive," and likened to a potato on matchsticks, due to the slender legs.

This physique seems to have been ignored by the creators of Ste-Cat, a mascot of the Montreal Jazz Festival in Canada. Ste-Cat is said to be a Chartreux, but the cartoons that appear on T-shirts show a truly bright blue cat made up of musical notes; the slender legs are still there, but on the way she seems to have lost a lot around the midriff and acquired a rather more Oriental face.

TRUE TO TYPE Old photographs highlight the sheen of the coat and the smile so typical of the breed, which is due to its prominent, rounded whisker pads.

SLOW STARTER The Chartreux is far from a precocious breed. It can take two years or more to reach maturity, going through a gawky "teenage" stage.

In terms of personality, the Chartreux is a flâneur, an observer rather than an active participant in events. Its high, chirping voice is never used to excess, and while it is affectionate and can be playful, it needs personal space.

Grooming is minimal: Brushing is discouraged, but rubbing and stroking are recommended to bring out the best in the coat. There is a slight health concern with slipping kneecaps (patellar luxation); breeders should screen for this.

The naming of Chartreux cats is a curious matter. There is a convention that all kittens born in a particular year are given names starting with the same letter, although K, Q, W, X, Y, and Z are omitted from the sequence to save breeders' sanity.

Russian Shorthair

ORIGIN Russia (before 1800s)

SYNONYM Russian Blue, Foreign Blue, Maltese Cat, Spanish Blue, Archangel Cat

WEIGHT 7–12 lb. (3–5.5 kg.)

BUILD 🐈

TEMPERAMENT 🐱

COAT CARE 🖌

COLORS Blue, black, and white self only; blue self only in CFA

Considered a lucky cat in Russia, these cats or images of them were traditionally given to brides, perhaps as a charm to insure children. They may also have been put in new babies' cradles to drive out malign influences. This old and naturally occurring breed was Russia's first feline export, and a highly successful one.

BLACK SELF   WHITE   BLUE SELF

BREED ORIGINS

Rumors had it that the Russian Blue was the favored cat of the Russian Czars. Less romantic tales with more evidence on their side tell us they were valued for their skins. The old name of Archangel Cat alludes to their supposed origins around the Russian port of Archangel, and the tradition that these cats were brought to Britain by Russian sailors in the 1860s. The alternative names of Spanish Blue and Maltese Cat muddy the waters somewhat, but the Russian sailors seem to win in the credibility stakes.

The Russian Blue was shown at Crystal Palace in 1875 under the name Archangel Cat, and exported to the United States by 1900. Early breed work was concentrated in Europe. Today the breed is recognized by all the major registries, but there are some differences. In the 1970s, Australian breeder Mavis Jones created a Russian White, and a Russian Black has followed. These are recognized in Australia, New Zealand, and South Africa, and have preliminary status in the GCCF, but elsewhere resistance has seen them remain outside the fold. Because of this, the breed is known as the Russian or Russian Shorthair in some places and the Russian Blue in others; the GCCF lists the three colors separately.

OWNING A RUSSIAN

The Russian is generally semiforeign in type, with a lean, muscular, slightly

SILVER TIPPING The coat is hard to describe: the CFA standard calls for "distinctly silver tipped" guard hairs, the GCCF standard specifies no silver tipping, and FIFé settles for "a silver sheen."

Royal kitties?

It is sometimes claimed that Queen Victoria favored Russian Blues, but the same claim is also made on behalf of the British Shorthair and even the Chartreux. The first show classes pitted all blue cats against each other, and if the queen owned a blue cat it would be easy for anyone wanting the royal seal of approval to claim it was their breed that sat on the palace cushions. The Russian got its own class at British cat shows in 1912, but the public inclination to see all blue cats as one still exists today.

angular look. The original Russian is distinguished by the recessive blue coat. Early Russians shown in the United Kingdom had yellow eyes, and it was not until the 1930s that a green eye color was written into the breed standard.

The coat is silky and double. The GCCF standard describes it as "very different in texture from any other breed and the truest criterion of the Russian." It is tipped with silver, giving a sparkling, shimmering appearance.

Russians are easy to care for: Indeed, some breeders claim that the less the coat is groomed, the deeper its sheen will become. They are best suited to a quiet home without upheavals; while affectionate, they are dignified, quiet, slightly shy cats that do not appreciate too much hurly burly. They are unlikely to react aggressively to overmuch handling, but tend to wriggle away and seek quiet elsewhere, so can be a disappointing pet for children or others who want to cuddle a cat frequently. In all ways, this is a very grown-up breed.

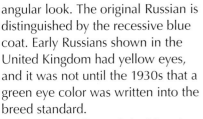

MONA LISA SMILE
Standards call for a moderately long, blunt wedge. The large ears are generally upright, the eyes almond shaped and widely spaced. The muzzle and whisker pads can give the cat a mysterious smile.

American Shorthair

ORIGIN United States (1900s)

SYNONYM Once called Domestic Shorthair

WEIGHT 8–15 lb. (3.5–7 kg.)

BUILD

TEMPERAMENT

COAT CARE

COLORS Western colors in self, tortie, bicolor, smoke, shaded, and tipped; blotched and striped tabby patterns

Although its name declares this no-nonsense breed to be the national American cat, it has been a less successful ambassador than the hugely popular Maine Coon. At home, it still enjoys a high profile, although other shorthaired breeds have overtaken it over the years.

BLACK SELF   BLACK & WHITE   RED STRIPED TABBY   SILVER STRIPED TABBY   TORTIE & WHITE   BLUE TORTIE & WHITE

BREED ORIGINS

Domestic cats have been present on the North American mainland for at least five centuries, since the first European settlers landed with their ships' cats. They spread across the continent just as the settlers did, although perhaps more slowly than dogs: A cat does not take easily to a shifting territory centered on a moving vehicle.

For the first four hundred years of American feline history, cats were simply working animals: Mousers protecting homes, farms, and businesses from rodents, just as they did the world over. They developed into large cats, the better to cope with the predators and prey on this new continent, with a thick, dense, and hard coat to keep out cold and moisture.

In the late 19th century, people began to show and breed cats, although at the start the definition of a breed was hazier and the rules about what kinds of cats were judged against each other much broader than they are in today's highly organized fancy. At the second cat show in Madison Square Garden, New York, in 1896, a brown tabby American Shorthair, not yet quite a breed, was offered for sale for $2,500. When the Cat Fanciers' Association (CFA) was established a decade later, the Domestic Shorthair was one of just five recognized breeds.

It was established by a cross in 1904 with the British Shorthair. British cats were regarded as higher quality than American cats, and crosses helped to strengthen desired traits by using lines that had already been selectively bred for some time.

Renamed American Shorthair in 1966, the breed remains in the top ten in the United States. The American fancy, however, seems to have a preference for longhaired and more exotic breeds, which claim the very top spots. Overseas, the breed is virtually unknown.

OWNING AN AMERICAN SHORTHAIR

This is a cat for those who want a breed still close to its working roots. With a breed standard that calls for no part "so exaggerated as to foster weakness," it is a robust, sturdy cat. In character, the American Shorthair is alert, intelligent, and friendly, tending more towards quiet companionship than demonstrative dependency.

SILVER CLASSIC TABBY It was when a cat of this color won the title of Cat of the Year that the breed name was changed from Domestic Shorthair to American Shorthair.

Antipodean

ORIGIN New Zealand and Australia (1990s)

SYNONYM Initially called New Zealand Shorthair

WEIGHT 8–15 lb. (3.5–7 kg.)

BUILD

TEMPERAMENT

COAT CARE

COLORS Western colors in self, tortie, bicolor, smoke, shaded, and tipped; all tabby patterns

The cat fancy began by recognizing national types as breeds—almost all of the early breeds had regional or national names. In the 20th century, much attention turned to creating breeds based on distinctive features instead. Around the world, however, breeds continue to crystalize out of national types.

BLACK SELF   RED & WHITE   BROWN CLASSIC TABBY   CREAM STRIPED TABBY   TORTIE & WHITE   TORTIE TABBY

BREED ORIGINS

One of the latest breeds to graduate from the class of domestic random breed is the Antipodean. This was at first called the New Zealand Shorthair, but the name was altered to reflect the work done by breeders in Australia, simultaneously giving the breed a broader base of appeal.

The Antipodean's ancestors arrived in the region with the Europeans. Nobody is quite sure when—it has been suggested that ships' cats were left on the Australian mainland before settlement—but certainly by the mid-18th century. The intervening century and a half has allowed time for generations of cats to breed and develop their own distinct type.

OWNING AN ANTIPODEAN

The type is moderate, muscular, and medium bodied, with a wedge shaped head that is neither elongated into a foreign type, nor shortened. While the climate in its homeland varies from cool, mountainous terrain to desert, no part of it is inhospitably cold; there is a longhaired version, but the shorthair is more often seen.

These are lively, intelligent and self-sufficient cats. Whether they catch the imagination or suffer the obscurity of other moderate breeds, such as the European Shorthair, remains to be seen.

HELPING HAND A robust type with a large initial gene pool, the Antipodean could be of use as an outcross for other breeds. Once a type is stabilized and all the genes known, it is attractive to other breeders as a known quantity.

Snowshoe

ORIGIN United States (1960s)

SYNONYM None

WEIGHT 6–12 lb. (2.5–5.5 kg.)

BUILD 🐈

TEMPERAMENT 🐆

COAT CARE 🪥

COLORS All colors in self and tortie (eumelanistic only in CFA); all tabby patterns (no tabby in CFA); always in pointed pattern and with white spotting

Beauty is truly in the eye of the beholder, and what some breeders scorn others will love. The white toes that were regarded as a fault in the early Siamese have been cherished as a distinctive feature in other breeds, and they even sparked the creation of the Snowshoe.

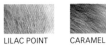
LILAC POINT

CARAMEL POINT

CHOCOLATE POINT

FAWN POINT

SEAL TABBY POINT

RED TABBY POINT & WHITE

BREED ORIGINS

Early Siamese breeders in the West tried to eradicate the genes behind the white toes or paws that sometimes appeared in their kittens. In the 1950s, some American breeders tried to reverse this trend and create a white-footed Siamese under the attractive name of Silver Laces, but their efforts faded into obscurity. Then in the 1960s, Philadelphia breeder Dorothy Hinds-Daugherty noticed white feet in Siamese kittens and attempted to stabilize the "fault" into a feature. After much frustration, the Siamese were crossed with American Shorthairs, giving a reliable bicolor trait, and the Snowshoe was on its way.

BICOLOR In TICA, a cat with an inverted "V" of white on its face is a bicolor. Less than two thirds of the coat, on the lower half, should be white.

There was, naturally enough, opposition to the very existence of the Snowshoe from some Siamese breeders, who had spent decades reducing the appearances of white feet. This was also the first shorthaired cat breed to adopt the pointing pattern that was virtually the trademark of the Siamese, and the possibility of confusion in the public mind caused concern. The longhaired Birman had of course

SEAL MITTED A mitted Snowshoe may have any pattern of white except an inverted "V" in TICA; in the other registries, an inverted "V" is preferred.

had the pattern for decades, and the Snowshoe was for a time described as a shorthaired Birman. The Birman now has its own, genuine shorthaired counterpart in the Templecat.

OWNING A SNOWSHOE

The Snowshoe was originally quite similar to the Siamese in looks, although a little more solid due to the American Shorthair input. As the Siamese has become more slender and elongated, the two have diverged until nobody could confuse them.

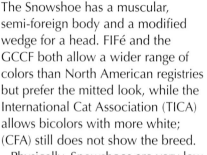

The Snowshoe has a muscular, semi-foreign body and a modified wedge for a head. FIFé and the GCCF both allow a wider range of colors than North American registries but prefer the mitted look, while the International Cat Association (TICA) allows bicolors with more white; (CFA) still does not show the breed.

Physically, Snowshoes are very low maintenance. The coat is single, like that of Oriental breeds, and needs

KITTENS Like all pointed cats, Snowshoe kittens are born white. The breeder must wait some weeks to be sure of the coat patterns that will emerge.

no day-to-day care. This is a healthy breed, with no major inherited problems or physiological weaknesses.

The Snowshoe shows its Oriental heritage in more than just its coat. It is a playful, outgoing breed, and easily bored: not the best choice for someone who wants to leave a snoozing pet alone for much of the day. Snowshoes are gregarious, and a two-cat household may work better than a lone cat. They can also be talkative, but have a softer voice than some Oriental breeds, making them ideal for those who like a responsive pet but don't want one that will talk their ears off.

LILAC TABBY MITTED The most liberal registry of all with regard to colors and pattern, FIFé recognizes tabby patterns in the Snowshoe. Like all colors, the difference between the body and point colors is strong.

Asians

ORIGIN United Kingdom (1981)
SYNONYM Smokes were called Burmoires
WEIGHT 9–15 lb. (4–7 kg.)
BUILD
TEMPERAMENT
COAT CARE
COLORS Western and Eastern colors in self, tortie, smoke, and shaded; tabby and sepia patterns

The Asians are distinguished as a group, rather than a single breed, by the GCCF registry. This reflects the fact that, although the cats share a common ancestry and type, the coats and the rules about what is allowed for each coat type are perhaps more diverse than for any other breed.

| WHITE | BLUE TICKED TABBY | RED TICKED TABBY | SILVER SHADED | LILAC POINT | FAWN POINT |

BREED ORIGINS

The origin of the Asian breed group lies in the accidental mating of two distinguished breeds. Breeder Miranda Bickford-Smith (née von Kirchberg) had bought a chinchilla Persian. The Persian was due to be neutered, but in the kind of mishap that owners are always warned about, he met a lilac Burmese and insured the survival of his line before human intervention.

The resulting litter of four female kittens had the Burmese type but sparkling silver-shaded coats. Their appearance and temperament were striking enough for the Persian male to be given a second chance with

another Burmese, resulting in a male kitten, and a breeding program followed, outcrossing to Burmese to increase the gene pool.

The initial name of Burmilla for these shaded cats was a natural "portmanteau" from Burmese and chinchilla. The GCCF initially

ROOM FOR CONFUSION Black Asian selfs are called Bombays, but are completely unrelated to the American breed of the same name.

recognized the Burmilla, officially called the Asian Shaded, in 1989, and also shows all the other coats in the group. FIFé recognized the Burmilla alone in 1994; under FIFé breed standards, the breed is also being developed in Australia.

CHOCOLATE TABBY This blotched tabby shows the sepia pattern, with the markings on the body gently faded.

CHOCOLATE SMOKE The ideal smoke Asian appears solid colored when still, with the white undercoat only revealed in movement.

BLACK SILVER SHADED Shaded cats may have a creamy "standard" or pure white "silver" undercoat. Any degree of tipping is allowed.

TORTIE The GCCF recognizes all possible colors in Asian Selfs including the "dilute modifier" shades and five torties, giving 13 in total.

OWNING AN ASIAN

All Asians are similar in type to the European Burmese, with a muscular, lithe body and medium legs and tail, all cloaked in a fine, short, sleek coat. The head is a relatively short wedge, with gently curved planes, and medium to large, fairly tall ears that are angled slightly out. The eyes are large and intermediate in shape—between rounded and oval. The range of coats, however, is much wider than in the Burmese.

The first generation of crosses always produced cats with short and shaded coats, because these dominant genes masked the sepia pointing of the Burmese and the long coat of the Persian. Later generations saw new coats emerging: Longhaired, self, smoke, sepia patterned, and even tabby, because any shaded cat is genetically an agouti. The selfs and the tabbies had to content themselves with the relatively plain labels of Asian Selfs and Asian

Tabbies, but the smokes were for a time called Burmoires and the longhairs are known as Tiffanies.

Asians are healthy and easy to care for; their coats need little routine grooming. But this cat first appealed to breeders for its temperament as much as its looks. While all show standards call for aggression or other undesirable behavior in the show ring to be penalized, this was the first cat to include points for temperament in the breed standard. Livelier and more inquisitive than the typical Persian personality, Asians stop short of the fulltilt inquisitiveness and attention seeking of the pure-blooded Burmese. Truly the best of both worlds, they make easygoing, friendly companions with a relaxed outlook on life.

The long haul

The journey to recognition can be a protracted one, with many stages. First, cats' pedigrees are recorded in a stage that may be called Preliminary or Miscellaneous, with cats exhibited at shows, but not competing. After this comes a stage often called Provisional, where cats compete against each other but perhaps not against other breeds. Only at what is usually called Championship level is a breed "fully" accepted. Asians were registered by the GCCF from 1989, but only achieved Championship status in 1997.

LILAC This is the most common tabby pattern in the Asian. This is because most Burmese cats in the United Kingdom carry two copies of the ticked gene.

Seychellois

ORIGIN Europe (2000s)

SYNONYM None

WEIGHT 9–14 lb. (4–6.5 kg.)

BUILD

TEMPERAMENT

COAT CARE

COLORS All solid eumelanistic colors except dilute modifier shades in self and tortie; red and cream in tabby patterns; always with white; always in pointed pattern

When is a breed not a breed? When it is a color or pattern in another breed. The Oriental breeds have between them stirred up enough international naming anomalies to confuse everyone for years. And it isn't over yet: This European breed is an example of registry independence for the new millennium.

RED TABBY POINT & WHITE

BLUE POINT

LILAC POINT

CHOCOLATE POINT

FAWN POINT

SEAL BICOLOR There are three different classes of coat: the bicolor, the harlequin, and the van. All have color on the head and tail; the harlequin also has color on the legs, and the bicolor has color on the legs and body.

BREED ORIGINS

The Seychellois looks like a Siamese in a bicolor coat, and that is pretty much what it is. These are included in the Oriental Shorthair and Longhair by CFA and TICA, but not in Europe.

In the 1980s, British geneticist Pat Turner set out to achieve cats of Oriental type in a white coat with patches of color and a solid-colored tail, working with another breeder, Julie Smith. In 1988, they showed two cats auspiciously named Victoria and Félicité.

Getting colors recognized within an existing breed is often harder than getting a new breed recognized. Clearly these cats would not be accepted as Siamese: Siamese breeders have devoted decades to getting rid of the spotting gene, and did not want it back. Recognition within the Oriental Shorthair was also resisted—GCCF did not even recognize bicolored Orientals. And so FIFé has given these cats the name Seychellois, in reference to the cats of the Seychelles said to have inspired the breed, but also following the tradition of using the names of islands for offshoots of the Siamese, as in the Balinese and Javanese. In the United Kingdom, the GCCF has instead started the process of recognition for Oriental bicolors and includes the pointed colors within this, following the U.S. lead.

OWNING A SEYCHELLOIS

The Seychellois is typically Oriental, ideal for those who want a new twist on that elongated face, slender body, and long legs. There is a longhair as well as the shorthair but, like the Balinese and the Oriental Longhair, the difference is seen mostly in a plumelike tail and a neck ruff.

While the official Seychellois breed is likely to remain a European idiosyncrasy, those smitten with the patchwork look can find pointed Oriental bicolors elsewhere. They are easy to run, with minimal grooming and health problems, and described by breeders as sensitive, athletic, loving, and demonstrative.

American Burmese

ORIGIN Burma, now Myanmar (before 1930s)

SYNONYM Some colors once called Mandaly

WEIGHT 8–14 lb. (3.5–6.5 kg.)

BUILD 🐈

TEMPERAMENT 🐆

COAT CARE 🪥

COLORS All colors in self and tortie in TICA (sable, blue, chocolate, and lilac only in CFA); always in sepia pattern

The Burmese breed has had a short but eventful history. Although it only arrived in the West well into the 20th century, within 50 years it split into two distinct types. This distinctly round-headed type is one of them: The other, with a more wedge-shaped head, is the European Burmese.

LILAC POINT   CHOCOLATE POINT   FAWN POINT

The head fault

The lines of American show champion Good Fortune Fortunatus, now found on almost every pedigree, carry a gene for a severe malformation called the Burmese craniofacial deformity. There is one lower jaw but two upper muzzles and noses, the eyes and ears are deformed, and the top of the head is incomplete, with a bulging brain covered by skin but no skull. Geneticists have identified the chromosome and the area of it that is responsible for the deformity: They hope they are close to finding the gene and developing a genetic test to allow the fault to be bred out. Until then, kittens die at birth or must be euthanized.

SABLE The look of the American Burmese is summed up by the words compact and rounded. Sable is genetically black degraded by the sepia gene.

BREED ORIGINS

The defining characteristic of all Burmese is the sepia pattern. This was widespread throughout southeast Asia: The copper colored Thong Daeng in the historic Thai *Cat Book Poems* or *Tamra Maew* are probably Burmese.

The mother of the breed was Wong Mau, brought to the United States in 1930. She was a natural Tonkinese; mated to a Siamese she produced pointed and mink kittens. Only when bred to one of the latter did she produce sepia pattern Burmese.

The breed's early history was turbulent: It was first recognized by CFA and then demoted in the 1930s. Reinstated in the 1950s, it had a new look and breed standard by the 1970s, when cats with a very rounded, short-muzzled head won all the prizes. This "contemporary" head is now the standard look of the American Burmese, but it carries a price (*see* box).

OWNING A BURMESE

It may look sleek, but that muscular body is surprisingly heavy; the classic description is "bricks wrapped in silk." The glossy silk of the coat is fine and flat, without an undercoat, and virtually maintenance free. Burmese are less vocal than many of the other Oriental breeds but still absurdly gregarious and affectionate.

European Burmese

ORIGIN Burma, now Myanmar (before 1930s)

SYNONYM Red colors called Foreign Burmese in Canada

WEIGHT 8–14 lb. (3.5–6.5 kg.)

BUILD

TEMPERAMENT

COAT CARE

COLORS Brown, blue, chocolate, lilac, red, and cream in self and tortie; always in sepia pattern

There are essentially two separate Burmese breeds, each referred to in their respective homelands simply as Burmese. The European type is now shown in North America, but the American type is not bred or shown abroad. This was one of the first breeds to suffer a schism over type, although others show signs of following in its footsteps.

LILAC POINT

CHOCOLATE POINT

FAWN POINT

BREED ORIGINS

The European Burmese was originally the same breed as the American Burmese. The breed was recognized in the United Kingdom in 1952 in the original brown color. After this, the breed diverged until it had two completely different looks: One in the United States and one in Europe. More colors were recognized in the European Burmese, and eventually differences over the shape of the head and health issues led to American cats being barred from European breeding lines.

The split between the American and the European versions of this breed began in 1959, when CFA revised their standard for the Burmese, requiring a round head with a short muzzle. European breeders, on the other hand, kept a generally "foreign" type, with a wedge-shaped head. The issue became more urgent in the 1970s, when the "contemporary" look took hold in the United States. Because of the lethal gene carried in the lines

associated with this look, Burmese from American lines that might carry the fault cannot even be registered in the GCCF and many other associations.

OWNING A BURMESE

The European breed is characterized by the sepia pattern, with color shading softly from dark points to a lighter body. A wide range of colors has been developed and is recognized in the European

LILAC TORTIE Torties arrived in the Burmese in the 1960s, at first through an accidental mating, followed by a planned cross.

CHOCOLATE This color was brought into the European Burmese from cats imported from the United States in the late 1960s, when the two types still interbred.

Burmese, but no shaded forms or tabby patterns.

The wedge-shaped head is the most obvious factor distinguishing the European from the American Burmese, but the differences extend to other aspects of the build as well. The legs are slender, but still strong in appearance, and the tail is medium in thickness and the same length as the body. The body is lean, but a dense, muscular build makes these cats heavier than they look. All this is wrapped in a fine, short coat that lies flat against the body, with no insulating undercoat to pad it out.

The Burmese is a low-maintenance breed, generally sound in health and needing no day-to-day care to keep it sleek and glossy. In personality, it is a gregarious and active companion, which is well suited to either a family home or a household with more than one cat. It is less vocal and inquisitive than the breeds derived from the Siamese, however, and makes a peaceable choice for those who find chattier Oriental types a bit overwhelming.

LILAC This dilute of chocolate, a pale, pink-tinged gray, was developed in the 1970s. Green eyes are a fault, but the eye color changes in different lights.

Tonkinese

ORIGIN United States and Canada (1960s)
SYNONYM Tonkanese, Golden Siamese
WEIGHT 6–12 lb. (2.5–5.5 kg.)
BUILD
TEMPERAMENT
COAT CARE
COLORS All colors except cinnamon and fawn in self and tortie (only eumelanistic in CFA); all tabby patterns (not in CFA or TICA); always mink

The pattern that defines the Tonkinese had been in existence long before the breed itself was recognized—or created, depending on your point of view. This breed was a first in the feline world because it was accepted from the start as an inevitable part of its genetic makeup that it would never breed true.

LILAC POINT   CARAMEL POINT   CHOCOLATE POINT   FAWN POINT   SEAL TABBY POINT

BREED ORIGINS

The Tonkinese is a hybrid of the Siamese and the Burmese. Two mutations of the same gene are responsible for the different pointing patterns seen in these breeds, but neither form is dominant over the other. The result is that if a cat carries one copy of each form (a state called heterozygous), it will show an intermediate pattern that is less dramatically pointed than the Siamese, but more pointed than the Burmese: This is the distinguishing pattern of the Tonkinese, which is known as mink.

It is possible that some of the unacceptably dark "chocolate Siamese" mentioned in British sources of the 1880s may have been minks. But the very first Tonkinese reliably recorded in the West was in fact Wong Mau, the founder of the Burmese breed. When bred to a

Siamese, she produced kittens of a Siamese coat type (showing she carried the pointing gene) and kittens of her own type (showing she carried the sepia gene). Only when she was mated to one of her kittens with the same coat as herself did she produce the all sepia Burmese.

In the 1950s breeders deliberately recreated this hybrid as the Golden Siamese in the United States, and then in the 1960s as the Tonkinese in Canada, where it was finally recognized. Today it is accepted by most major registries; efforts to create a longhair under the name Silkanese or Himbur have come to nothing.

Because both forms of the mutation are needed in any Tonkinese meeting the breed standard, a litter of kittens from two Tonkinese will inevitably include some pointed and some sepia types;

LILAC TORTIE The mixture of colors in the tortie coat tends to obscure the shading of the mink pattern, even more so with dilute shades.

TICA and CFA show these, but not the GCCF. Most breeders seek to eliminate variants and breed true to the standard, so the fact that this is impossible in the Tonkinese has led some people to question whether it is a breed at all.

CHOCOLATE Mixing two breeds with different characteristics leaves some undesirable traits. Eyes from blue to green are accepted in minks, but golden eyes only in sepia cats.

OWNING A TONKINESE

Whatever the misgivings of the pedants, the Tonkinese has become a popular breed, although it lurks outside the top ten that are annually recorded in the United Kingdom and United States. Indeed, it is a very attractive cat: Less angular than one parent but more lithe than the other, with a unique eye color that is described as "aqua."

They are affectionate and lively cats, always on the move through the home, and remarkably tolerant of even the unpredictable nature of children's play. They have melodious voices that are used in moderation.

BLUE The blue of the Tonkinese is allowed to have warm undertones, rather than the crisp, cool color seen in some other breeds.

RED The distinctions between Siamese and Tonkinese coats can be blurred by polygenetic factors and climate.

CHOCOLATE TORTIE The base color should be a warm chocolate, well broken up with varying shades of red, which should show no tabby markings.

Siamese (including Colorpoint Shorthair)

ORIGIN Siam, now Thailand (before 1800s)
SYNONYM Once called Royal Cat of Siam
WEIGHT 6–12 lb. (2.5–5.5 kg.)
BUILD
TEMPERAMENT
COAT CARE

COLORS All colors in self and tortie (some called Colorpoint Shorthair in CFA); all tabby patterns (called Colorpoint Shorthair in CFA); always in pointed pattern

As if its extraordinary looks were not enough to get it noticed, the Siamese arrived in Europe embellished with tales of both a royal heritage and a past as a sacred temple cat. In fact, the Siamese has probably had more extravagant legends attached to it than any other breed in feline history.

RED POINT   CREAM POINT   BLUE TABBY POINT   LILAC TABBY POINT

BREED ORIGINS

The mutation that causes the pointed coat pattern arose at least five centuries ago, somewhere in Asia, and it was most strongly associated with the Far East: Beyond these generalities, nothing specific has yet been ascertained.

Cats of Siamese type appear in Thai manuscript books. The original *Tamra Maew*, or *Cat Book Poems*, was compiled sometime between 1350 and 1767, and a new *Smud Khoi* copy was made from the old texts between 1868 and 1910. In these texts, the Siamese is called the Wichien-Maat (the translated spellings vary).

BLUE POINT The dilute gene that gives the blue color may well have come west as a hidden trait in the very first cats imported.

SEAL POINT Today's Siamese breed standards call for deep blue eyes, strikingly large ears, and long legs and tail.

Despite trade between West and East for centuries, no record of Siamese pointed cats reaching the West can be found before the 19th century. In 1879, the American Consul in Bangkok brought cats to the United States from Thailand, and in 1884, the British Vice Consul in Bangkok sent a breeding pair back to Britain as a gift for his sister, Lilian Jane Veley. Although the story goes that these cats were a royal gift, and they were dubbed the Royal Cats of Siam, no real evidence has been found to back up this romantic tale.

These two cats and their three kittens were shown at the Crystal Palace Show in 1885. Their exotic appearance and emphatic voices were not a hit with everybody. However, enough people were taken with them for this line to become the start of the Siamese breed in Europe.

Breed standards or buyer's guide?

The *Tamra Maew* is rather like a field guide to cats. Verses accompanying each cat's picture give details of the coat and type very similar to a modern breed standard. In some cases they also outline the cat's behavior, and how one should behave towards the cat. There is no reference to breeding as such, only advice to seek out the desirable types. And not all are desirable: There are evil, bad-luck cats to avoid. These often look as if they have congenital or other health problems, and their texts could be seen as simple husbandry advice.

OWNING A SIAMESE
Self cats were excluded in the 1920s, eventually becoming the Oriental Shorthairs. Unwanted longhairs became the Balinese. When "new" colors appeared, not all associations accepted them; CFA still calls them Colorpoint Shorthairs. But the most controversial change is more subtle. The Siamese has become "ultra typed"—extremely slender. In response, TICA began the process in 2007 of recognizing a less etiolated type under the name of Thai.

On one level, Siamese are fairly low maintenance, with a fine, short coat that needs no grooming. The lack of an undercoat and insulating fat means an outdoor lifestyle in a cooler climate may not be suitable.

SIAMESE KITTENS All pointed cats come out of the warmth of their mother's body completely white and will develop their points over the first few months.

But in personality, this is a high-maintenance pet. Vocal, sticking its long nose into everything, playful, and gregarious, the Siamese is the original all-singing, all-dancing party animal.

CHOCOLATE POINT This is one of the four colors first established in the breed: Chocolate, seal, and their dilute forms of lilac and blue.

CHOCOLATE TORTIE POINT Chocolate and lilac may have been carried from the start, with chocolates explained as "poor" seals.

APRICOT TABBY POINT This is the modified dilute form of red, and one of the later colors to be understood and recognized in many cats.

Oriental Shorthair

ORIGIN United Kingdom (1950s)

SYNONYM Once called Foreign Shorthair in Britain

WEIGHT 9–14 lb. (4–6.5 kg.)

BUILD

TEMPERAMENT

COAT CARE

COLORS All colors in self, tortie, smoke, shaded, and tipped; all tabby patterns

Burdened with a multitude of names down the decades, Oriental cats have suffered a few identity crises since they first appeared in the West. But, despite it all, today they hover in or just outside the top ten breeds in both the United Kingdom and the United States, and hold their own elsewhere.

BLACK SELF | WHITE | LILAC STRIPED TABBY | RED TICKED TABBY | RED STRIPED TABBY & WHITE | BLUE TORTIE TABBY & WHITE

RED SELF It took a long time for this color to be accepted, because of the markings exposed by the red gene. Markings are now accepted in the color.

BREED ORIGINS

These solid-colored cats were at first included within the Siamese breed. But in the 1920s the Siamese Club of Great Britain changed the standard, deciding that the name Siamese excluded "any but blue-eyed" cats.

Numbers of these now unrecognized cats declined, until a European revival in the early 1950s succeeded in developing a chocolate self cat of foreign type. This was initially (and again later) known as Havana, but it was first recognized in 1958 in the United Kingdom as the Chestnut Brown Foreign. This cat contributed to the development of the Havana Brown breed in the United States, but the two are quite separate. In the United Kingdom, this was the start of the Foreigns, the name given to all the self colored cats at first. In the

LILAC SELF Carried as a recessive gene by many cats used in developing the Havana, lilac was shown as "any other variety," together with blacks and blues until 1977.

1970s, Foreigns were accepted in CFA and other American registries, under the name Oriental Shorthair.

In the United Kingdom, tabbies were accepted in the late 1970s, but under the name of Orientals. At the start of the 1990s, almost all Foreigns were rechristened Oriental Shorthairs in the United Kingdom, removing some confusion. In the United States, CFA classes the shorthairs and the longhairs as one breed with two divisions, an approach that has not been taken up by other registries. The status of bicolors varies internationally.

OWNING AN ORIENTAL SHORTHAIR

The Oriental Shorthair head is a long, triangular wedge, topped by large ears that flare outward at an angle. The eyes, in vivid shades of clear, unflecked green, are slanted and widely set. The coat, like that of the Siamese, is short, fine, and lacking an insulating undercoat; this is not a cold-weather breed.

Oriental Shorthairs are long lived and generally healthy, although there is a tendency to heart attacks. They need no routine maintenance of the coat, although brushing it to a shine can be a pleasure for both owner and cat.

The Oriental personality reflects its ancestry. It loves nothing so much as to be the center of attention. It also has a loud voice, used liberally to remind you of its needs: Attention and plenty of activity.

BLUE SELF Blue cats of Siamese descent produced during development of the Havana color were registered as Russian Blues in the 1950s.

SILVER SHADED Recognition of shaded Orientals in the United Kingdom took 18 years from 1978. It was feared that the varied expression of the silver gene would lead to unpredictable coats.

Havana Brown

ORIGIN United Kingdom and United States (1950s)

SYNONYM Once called Chestnut Brown Foreign in United Kingdom

WEIGHT 6–10 lb. (2.5–4.5 kg.)

BUILD

TEMPERAMENT

COAT CARE

COLORS Chocolate self only

This is one of a handful of single-color breeds in the world. These cats can have a hard time winning fans: You have to love not just the type but the one coat color available, and none of these breeds make regular appearances in the top ten breeds. The Havana Brown is further hampered by confusion with an ancestor of the same name, and remains virtually unknown beyond the United States.

BREED ORIGINS

Brown cats were known and shown in Europe as far back as the late 19th century. Some of these were solid-colored Siamese, but the name "Swiss Mountain Cat" was also used. When these solid-colored cats were barred from the Siamese breed, they soon faded from view and almost from existence.

In the 1950s, they were taken up again by breeders in the United Kingdom, starting with a self brown termed the Havana—a genetic chocolate eventually recognized in the United Kingdom as the Chestnut Brown Foreign. In the mid-1950s, one of these cats was imported into the United States by a Mrs. Elsie Quinn. Other imports and breedings followed, and by 1959 a Havana Brown won Grand Champion status in CFA. While the Foreigns in the United Kingdom were bred to a more angular standard and became in general a solid-colored counterpart to the Siamese, eventually becoming the Oriental Shorthair, the American breed retained a more moderate, sweet-faced look. It could not now be confused with the British cat when seen, only by the name of the color.

OWNING A HAVANA BROWN

As a shorthair with a thin coat, the Havana Brown is as low maintenance as a breed can get—in terms of grooming, anyway. Their insatiable curiosity and playful nature can be harder to keep up with.

However, finding a Havana Brown may be a problem. Known only in North America, it is close to the bottom of the rankings in numbers of cats registered each year. Outcrosses were closed in the 1970s, and appeals to allow them again fell on deaf ears within CFA for some time. Although limited outcrossing is now once again underway, the breed still teeters on the brink of viability.

HAVANA FACE The head is a moderate wedge, with a distinctively rounded, somewhat narrow muzzle with a pronounced break.

HAVANA BROWN Every hair, including the whiskers, is a warm, even shade of brown. The shade is a rich mahogany, brighter and warmer than chocolate in some other breeds.

Bombay

ORIGIN United States (1960s)
SYNONYM None
WEIGHT 6–11 lb. (2.5–5 kg.)
BUILD 🐈
TEMPERAMENT 🐈
COAT CARE 🪥
COLORS Black self only

The desire to breed a domestic cat that resembles one of its wild brethren may seem like a new phenomenon, but in fact such ideas have a long history in the cat fancy. The Bombay, designed to be a "mini black panther," was the first of these attempts to win any serious recognition. While it looks relatively tame compared with some of the creations and even hybrids that have followed since, this was the pioneer of the class.

BREED ORIGINS

In the 1950s, Nikki Horner, a breeder from Kentucky, set out to create a domestic cat resembling a melanistic leopard. Starting with a black American Shorthair with deep copper eyes and a show-winning sable Burmese with a fine, glossy coat, she was disappointed with a lack of progress at first. A change in breeding lines provided better

BOMBAY BUILD The conformation of the Bombay is fairly close to that of the Burmese, with a substantial, muscular body, and a well-rounded chest.

Eye color

The Bombay breed standards call for brilliant copper eyes, but this is a hard color to achieve, and many must settle for gold instead. Eye color can vary considerably, not just across the breed but in the lifetime of an individual cat. Full, intense color can take some time to develop in kittens, and then it may fade or even gradually become greenish, particularly in male cats, once they reach maturity at three to five years.

results, and she succeeded in her aim by the 1960s.

The Bombay caught the eye of breeders and the public, and was recognized in North America during the 1970s. However, it has now been eclipsed by more recent arrivals, has never won widespread popularity abroad, and remains unrecognized by European registries. There is room for confusion in the United Kingdom, where the name Bombay is used for the black self color within the Asian breed group.

Outcrossing to the parent breeds is still allowed, but this is usually to Burmese for the desired conformation; the dominant black color of the American Shorthair needs no reinforcing. The recessive Burmese sepia gene means sable variants are still produced. One drawback of this outcrossing is that Bombay lines carry the lethal Burmese head fault.

OWNING A BOMBAY

Bombays have been described as the perfect cat for anyone who wants a dog—or a monkey. Showing their Oriental origins, they are gregarious, playful, and outgoing, and some owners successfully train them to fetch or to walk on a leash. They are heat seekers, and find no seat so

ROUNDED OR WEDGE Standards vary between CFA and TICA. Cats with a head shape closer to the European Burmese might do well in TICA but be heavily marked down in CFA.

INTENSE CONTRAST The Bombay should have a coat like black patent leather, with copper eyes shining out of it. The glossiness is due to a fine topcoat that lies flat, with no fluffy undercoat.

comfortable as the human lap. Their American Shorthair input tempers the Oriental side of their nature, making them self-reliant and laid back.

Abyssinian

ORIGIN Ethiopia (1800s)

SYNONYM None

WEIGHT 9–17 lb. (4–7.5 kg.)

BUILD

TEMPERAMENT

COAT CARE

COLORS All colors in self, tortie, and shaded (brown, blue, cinnamon, and fawn only in CFA); always in ticked tabby pattern

Distinguished by the ticked tabby pattern, this was for many decades the only cat for which the pattern was essential. Only with the arrival of the Singapura did the field widen. But for those seeking the translucent shimmer of the ticked coat with the look of the wild, the Abyssinian is still the breed of choice.

BLUE TICKED TABBY

RED TICKED TABBY

BROWN TICKED TABBY

BREED ORIGINS

The history of this striking breed is something of a riddle. It may come from Abyssinia (now Ethiopia), as its name implies, but it may not. Certainly cats of this type were brought back from Africa to the United Kingdom by returning troops. The founder of the cat fancy, Harrison Weir, wrote a breed standard in 1889. These early records should put the Abyssinian among the oldest known breeds.

But then the trail disappears. No recorded pedigree traces the later ticked cats back to the earliest imports, and the early pedigrees, going back as far as 1896, show mostly one or both parents as unknown. However, some also show crosses to other cats, which gives weight to the belief held by some breeders that the Abyssinian was in fact a British native masquerading as an exotic foreigner, actually created from crosses of existing silver and

BLUE The darker bands of slate-blue ticking alternate with beige, producing a warm dark blue coat, with very subtle shading.

LILAC This color is allowed by TICA and the GCCF only. The coat is of warm, pinkish cream ticked with pinkish dove-gray.

SORREL The second color to be recognized, this is also called red, but is genetically a cinnamon, not pheomelanistic red.

brown tabbies with native British ticked cats. The crosses do explain some of the recessive colors that surfaced later in the breed, not to mention the gene for long hair that eventually led to the creation of the Somali. However, the ticked pattern is not a European one; it may have been in the British feline population by this time, but it must have arrived from somewhere. Genetic studies have shed some light on the business: It is most probable that the ancestors of the modern Abyssinian, and the origin of the ticked tabby gene, came from Southeast Asia and the coast of the Indian Ocean.

After its early success at the London shows, the Abyssinian faded from view, and it barely existed as a breed by the turn of the 20th century. In the 1930s, after the founding of a dedicated breed club in the United Kingdom, top-quality cats sent overseas formed the foundation of a successful breeding program and the Abyssinian was established as a breed on both sides of the Atlantic, as well as in Australia and New Zealand. Unfortunately for British breeders, World War II put paid to cat showing and breeding, and by the end of the war there were only a dozen or so surviving Abys.

Although importing cats has helped the breed recover, it has never achieved the same levels of popularity in the United Kingdom as it has in the United States, where it consistently sits somewhere in the middle of the top ten breeds.

SILVER BLUE All the major associations except CFA accept and show the silver colors.

OWNING AN ABY

The ticked pattern is a dominant tabby gene. Beneath the subtle ticked coat there may be self or striped, blotched, or spotted tabby genes. The first color recognized in the breed was a brown tabby, given the name of "usual," unique to the Abyssinian breed. This is a dominant color, and beneath it there can be the genes for blue, chocolate, or cinnamon, and their dilute versions.

The Aby, while low maintenance, does have a few health problems. A pyruvate kinase (PK) deficiency causing intermittent anemia is carried as a recessive trait; there is a genetic test. Patellar luxation or slipping kneecaps, renal amyloidosis (deposits in the kidneys), and retinal atrophy (causing impaired vision) may also be found.

This is a people-oriented cat, but not a lap cat: It doesn't want to sit on you so much as play with you or, failing that, follow you around and "help you out." They are intelligent and loyal, and very curious.

CHOCOLATE Like its dilute, lilac, this is a relative latecomer to the Aby palette. The base coat is apricot, ticked with bands of dark chocolate to give an impression of a rich copper-brown.

Singapura

ORIGIN Singapore and United States (1970s)

SYNONYM The Malay word *Kucinta* ("sweet little cat") is sometimes used

WEIGHT 4–9 lb. (2–4 kg.)

BUILD 🐈

TEMPERAMENT 🐈

COAT CARE 🖌

COLORS Brown ticked tabby in sepia pattern only

This is one of those breeds that provoked a flurry of excited publicity, which in turn brought not a little grumpiness from breeders weary of the public appetite for novelty. And there was a little bit of cloak and dagger to the story of the Singapura's origins. As time has passed, other novelties have distracted the crowd, but these charming, small cats have become an established, if minority, interest in the cat world.

BREED ORIGINS

Singapura is the Malay name for the island of Singapore. The original breeders and champions of the Singapura, Hal and Tommy Meadow, said that they brought three local cats back from Singapore in 1975, which were the foundation of the breed. These were said to be strays, and they were markedly smaller than cats found in the West. The three cats were named Ticle and Tes, male and female littermate kittens, and Puss'e, a young female. The Meadows presented the Singapura to CFA as a natural breed in 1981 and it was fully recognized by 1988.

However, Tommy had been a breeder of Abyssinians, Burmese, and Siamese since 1955, and as the Singapura was distinguished not only by its size, but also by the innate characteristics of two of these breeds, pointed questions were asked. Some concerned documents

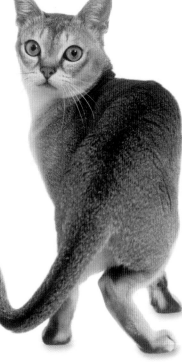

SMALL SIZE The smallest feline breed, Singapuras are still larger than the ferals of Singapore: Household cats are usually healthier and larger than ferals.

FACIAL MARKINGS The face is elegantly defined with dark brown eyeliner, lips, nose outline, and whisker roots. Dark lines extend over the brow and from the corners of the eyes.

SEPIA AGOUTI This combination is not the most commonly found coat pattern in Singapore, but it is still the only one allowed in the breed.

COMBINED PATTERNS Southeast Asia has the highest incidence of the ticked tabby gene, and the sepia trait was already known from Burma and possibly recorded in the Thai *Tamra Maew*.

showing that the Meadows had imported three cats into Singapore in 1974 that had the same names as those they brought back in 1975. In 1990 the CFA board looked into the issue and the Meadows admitted that Malay cats had been brought back earlier, without proper import papers. However, since the ticked tabby and sepia genes both originated from southeast Asia, and since another important Singapura ancestor was known to have come from a Singapore cat shelter, the Singapura breed was allowed to stand.

Having won recognition abroad, it has latterly caught the imagination back in Singapore. In 1990, the Singapore Tourist Promotion Board nominated the cat as a mascot, and held a "Name the Singapore River Cats" contest. The winner was *kucinta*, meaning "sweet little cat," a name that can, confusingly, be found on products bearing images of cats

with no resemblance to a Singapura. Life-size statues of cats and kittens now stroll and play among other sculptures along the Singapore River.

OWNING A SINGAPURA
The first issue when it comes to owning a Singapura is finding one. This breed has never achieved stellar popularity, and remains

rare, especially in Europe, where it is not recognized by FIFé.

If you obtain one, it will not be an overwhelming presence in your home. The Singapura is a quiet, retiring cat—said to be a relic of its feral evolution, where going unnoticed could save a lot of trouble. If a softly spoken, demure little cat is your aim, the Singapura may be for you.

KITTEN COATS The coat of the adult Singapura is single, silky, fine, and flat, but, like the correct yellow to green eye color, takes time to develop fully.

Korat

ORIGIN Siam, now Thailand (before 1800s)
SYNONYM Si-Sawat
WEIGHT 6–10 lb. (2.5–4.5 kg.)
BUILD
TEMPERAMENT
COAT CARE
COLORS Blue self only

It is said that a cat may look at a king, but few can claim to have been named by one. This ancient breed from Thailand claims just such a distinction, as well as a rainmaking role and one of the most poetic breed standards ever written. The Korat was a relative latecomer to the West, and remains something of a rarity, but in looks and personality this is a cat to remember.

BREED ORIGINS

The earliest record of the Korat is found in the Thai manuscript, the *Tamra Maew* or *Cat Book Poems* (1350–1767). This describes the silver-blue Si-Sawat: It was renamed Korat by King Chulalongkorn or Rama V (1853–1910) in order to commemorate the province of Thailand that is its homeland.

To call for rains in the Korat's homeland, a cat in a bamboo cage was paraded through the village; the cat was sprinkled with water, and then set free. Such ritualistic processions persisted into the 1980s, but rocket displays are now more favored. It is possible that the breed came to the West as early as the 19th century; a "blue Siamese" at an early show in London may have been either the type that became Oriental Shorthairs or a Korat. A more certain date is 1959, when Mrs. Jean Johnson brought Korats to the United States, where the breed was recognized by 1965. It was first brought to the United Kingdom in 1972, and was recognized by 1975.

OWNING A KORAT

The issue with a Korat is whether one owns it, or is owned by it. The large, rounded eyes and heart-shaped face look appealing and gentle, but this is an opinionated breed that will join in with whatever its owner is doing and then praise or criticize with equal enthusiasm. Whether with cats or people, the Korat wants to be top cat.

KORAT EYES The eyes should, according to the *Tamra Maew*, "shine like dewdrops on a lotus leaf."

COAT COLOR The *Tamra Maew*'s lyrical description says the coat is "as the flower of the pampas grass, smooth and orderly."

California Spangled

ORIGIN United States (1971)

SYNONYM None

WEIGHT 9–15 lb. (4–7 kg.)

BUILD 🐈

TEMPERAMENT 🐆

COAT CARE 🪮

COLORS Western colors in self, smoke, and silver in spotted tabby pattern only

Born from the mind of a Hollywood scriptwriter, this unusual and attractive cat should have had a happier ending. Arriving in a blaze of glory, today it is effectively a ghost breed. It blazed a trail, bringing wild-looking cats right to the forefront of public attention, but those who followed after trod more cautiously.

BROWN TABBY Spangles are registered by TICA, but not for competition. The breed standard allows white spotting on the chest, and "rosetted" groups of spots.

BREED HISTORY

In the 1970s, Californian Paul Casey was struck by the plight of wild cats hunted for their fur, and set out to create a wild-looking spotted cat, but without any wild blood. At the same time as he was developing his breed, Virginia Daly was working along similar lines in the Ocicat, but the stories couldn't have been more different. In the year when the Ocicat gained TICA recognition, Spangles were launched on the world—not through a cat show, but through the Neiman Marcus store catalogue.

SPANGLED BUILD The long, lean, muscular body is carried level on strong legs, giving a "hunter-like" quality to the cat's stride. Everything is meant to closely resemble a wild, natural cat.

THE BACKLASH

This move backfired in just about every way possible. The cat fancy was enraged that a "breed" developed without any outside observation of what had been done was being touted at premium prices. Campaigners were incensed that an "anti-fur" cat was for sale in a catalogue that included fur coats. Neiman Marcus themselves were less than pleased when they realized—apparently belatedly—that their furs were being criticized.

The Spangle never recovered from this disastrous start, and today it is mostly a reminder that a beautiful and even healthy cat is not enough for success. Breeding has been all but abandoned, although occasionally new interest leads to rumors of a return.

Egyptian Mau

ORIGIN Egypt and Italy (1950s)
SYNONYM None
WEIGHT 6–11 lb. (2.5–5 kg.)
BUILD
TEMPERAMENT
COAT CARE
COLORS Brown and silver in spotted tabby pattern, black smoke with "ghost" spotted tabby markings

The Egyptian Mau was the first breed to be defined by a spotted coat pattern; previous natural breeds had been defined by solid colors or pointing. Based on near-wild ancient cats, it was the first in a trend that persisted through the late 20th century, with the Ocicat bred to resemble a wild cat and then hybrid breeds including real wild blood.

BREED ORIGINS

Extreme romantics will claim that this breed dates back to the ancient Egyptian dynasties because it can trace its ancestry directly back to those cats. Of course, all cats' ancestry goes back to ancient Egypt: The Mau is simply the cat that stayed at home.

Deliberate breeding began with Nathalie Troubetskoy, an exiled Russian living in Italy after World War II. Struck by the appearance of spotted street cats in Cairo, she imported two and began breeding and showing the cats. She moved to the United States in 1956 and continued her work there. It took 20 years for the breed to win major recognition. Acceptance came latest in the United Kingdom, where early spotted Oriental Shorthairs had been called Maus; the naming conflict probably contributed to a lack of enthusiasm, and the breed was not recognized by the GCCF until after the turn of the century. It remains rare in Europe, although it is growing in popularity, and it sits somewhere in the middle of American breed rankings.

OWNING A MAU

The Mau has the looks of a natural cat from a warm climate. The long, athletic body is clad in fine, silky fur that lies close to

Egyptian ancestry

Mau is simply the Egyptian word for cat, descended directly from the very first name for the cat, *miu*, used in ancient Egyptian writings. It seems an apt name for a cat that resembles the depictions of cats in ancient wall paintings and scrolls more than any other modern feline. Such a look could have been recreated by careful choice of cats from anywhere in the world and a great deal of work, because all cats are descended from the same original Egyptian ancestors, and will carry those same original genes. But using street cats from Egypt undoubtedly gave the best chances of rapidly stabilizing the desired look, because unlike cats elsewhere, these descendants have not been subjected to the selection pressures of other environments that favored other adaptations alongside the original features. For example, there was no cold climate to favor the development of a dense undercoat, or more dramatically, a long topcoat.

SILVER The Mau comes in silver and smoke as well as bronze. The silver, seen here, is like all others, but uniquely, the smoke is a tabby with much less white undercoat than silver tabbies.

BRONZE This brown tabby coat is visually and genetically closest to the original cat at domestication. The eyes should be almond-shaped and gooseberry green in the mature cat.

the skin, but is not as short as that of Oriental breeds. Its head is a moderate wedge, defined by smooth curves with no flat planes, topped with medium to large, fairly upright ears.

The spots on the Mau, unlike those generally prized in cats of older breeds, do not follow the lines of a striped or mackerel tabby. The gene that is generally thought to be responsible for the spotted pattern can act on both striped and blotched patterns, and like the similarly spotted Ocicat, the Mau does throw classic or blotched tabby variants—a rather un-Egyptian trait. There is a whole range of other genes suggested that may have an effect on the pattern, however.

The short coat is easycare, and this is a robust breed. They have a soft, slightly chirping voice and friendly if busy natures. The Mau has a "belly flap" of skin at the back of the abdomen, which is generally not seen in pedigree breeds. It may not give a sleek line, but it nevertheless allows great extension of the body in a flat out gallop, and the active Mau will put it to use. This is a natural hunter: Owners who keep it indoors should be sure to provide suitable "prey"—before it chooses its own.

Ocicat

ORIGIN United States (1960s)

SYNONYM Ocelotte, Accicat

WEIGHT 6–14 lb. (2.5–6.5 kg.)

BUILD 🐈

TEMPERAMENT 🐾

COAT CARE 🖌

COLORS Eumelanistic colors in solid and silver spotted tabby pattern only

Breeding today often seems to be divided into those who treat genetic traits like a pick and mix counter, and create some very odd combinations, and those who disapprove of any changes or crossing of breeds. The Ocicat is the product of a less divided era, the accidental outcome of a dare between breeders that won over the world with ease.

BREED ORIGINS

The main difference between a pedigree breed and a lookalike random breed is what happens when the cat produces kittens. Breeds should "breed true," producing kittens like themselves—their type, coat, and color stabilized through generations of careful breeding. A lookalike cat can be a random coincidence, and just how diverse the results can be is shown by comparing the Ocicat with the Oriental Longhair. No immediate similarity is apparent, but the Ocicat comes from a cross identical to that which started the Oriental Longhair in the United Kingdom: A Siamese and an Abyssinian, with the aim of producing Siamese with ticked points. Virginia Daly, a breeder from Michigan, made the cross in the early 1960s, and in the second generation she got not only her hoped-for Aby-pointed Siamese but also selfs, classic tabbies, tabby points, and one spotted kitten, which Daly's daughter called an Ocicat. This was sold as a pet and neutered, but after communicating with Dr. Clyde Keeler of Georgia University, who wanted to produce a cat similar to the extinct Egyptian spotted fishing cat, Daly repeated the mating and a new breed was underway. Throughout the 1970s the breed was slow to develop, but interest was increasing. By the mid-1980s the Ocicat was recognized in CFA

SILVER SPOTTED The Ocicat head is ... wedge shaped, with a broad muzzle ... spaced, slightly slanted, almond-...s.

LILAC SILVER The silver gene was introduced into the breed quite early in its development through outcrosses to American Shorthairs, made by breeder Tom Brown.

and TICA. It started to spread around the world in the same decade, and is now recognized by all major international registries. Other wild-looking breeds followed, culminating in the hybrid Bengal.

OWNING AN OCICAT

The spotted tabby pattern of the Ocicat is the feature that first distinguished it. The spots do not follow the lines of the striped or mackerel tabby pattern, but the blotched or classic tabby. Blotched tabby, self, and smoke variants still appear. But the other vital element of the Ocicat's look is its muscular, powerful build. There is nothing cobby about the breed, but it is no lightweight built for elegant lounging: First and foremost it should resemble a wild cat.

The muscular body of the Ocicat is clothed in short, fine fur that needs no attention beyond the cat's own,

TAWNY This brown tabby color with large, well-scattered, oval spots is the original and classic Ocicat look, called tawny by CFA.

and this is a generally healthy breed, although inherited problems in the parent breeds may obviously also turn up in this breed. The wild looks are belied by a gregarious and playful personality, and Ocicats will follow owners around their homes apparently finding any activity interesting—this is definitely a cat that enjoys company.

CHOCOLATE All hairs except the tip of the tail are banded, tipped with a darker color in the markings, a lighter color elsewhere.

CLASSIC KITTEN Because its pattern is produced by the spotting gene breaking up the classic tabby pattern, blotched or classic tabby kittens like this are born.

Persian

ORIGIN United Kingdom (1800s)
SYNONYM Longhair, Himalayan
WEIGHT 8–15 lb. (3.5–7 kg.)
BUILD
TEMPERAMENT
COAT CARE

COLORS All colors and bicolors in all shades; all but ticked tabby pattern (not spotted in CFA); pointed pattern (also sepia and mink in TICA)

The first distinctive feature of the Persian is its luxurious coat, far longer than it was in the original cats brought from the East. The second distinctive feature is the short nose, which gives the breed a brachycephalic face described as "pansy-like" by its fans, but associated with breathing and eye problems.

BLUE SELF (LONG)

RED & WHITE

BLUE SILVER TABBY

BLACK SMOKE

SEAL POINT

BLUE POINT

BREED ORIGINS

Longhaired cats may have been brought to the West during the Crusades, but the first imports to be reliably recorded took place in the 17th century. Pietro della Valle brought longhaired cats from Persia to Italy, and Nicolas-Claude Fabri de Pieresc brought them from Turkey to France.

Persians were recognized by the cat fancy and given their own written standard in the late 19th century. However, the standards in both the United States and United Kingdom classed all types of longhaired cats as Longhairs, and each color as a separate breed. This has changed over the years, and now the breed, in all colors, is recognized by all major registries internationally and known by the Persian name everywhere.

Khmers and Himalayans

In the 1930s, American geneticists investigating coat patterns crossed Siamese cats with Persians. The resulting pointed longhairs were called Himalayans, after Himalayan rabbits with a similar pointing pattern, but were not pursued as a breed. In Europe there was a pointed longhair called the Khmer, and separate efforts were made to create a pointed Persian. The GCCF recognized the colorpoint pattern as part of the Persian breed in 1955, and the Khmer was absorbed into the group. Renewed interest in North America led to acceptance there by 1961, as the Himalayan.

CHOCOLATE TORTIE The Oriental range of colors naturally accompanied the pointed pattern. Because of the genetics, all-female torties must be created anew in each generation.

POINTED PERSIANS Persians like this lilac point have softer shading and lighter eyes than a Siamese.

All colors are now accepted internationally (under varied names), in solid, tortie, pointed, or bicolor, and smoke, shaded, and tipped.

In personality, the Persian is undemanding. It is quiet, sweet-voiced, and content to lounge around, although clipped cats are more active. The short face can cause breathing problems and kinked tear ducts, and there is a high incidence of polycystic kidney disease and retained testicles.

Persians have been seen as high status pets ever since they first appeared. It became the most popular breed in the United States by far in the 20th century and still leads by a four to one margin, although its star has faded elsewhere.

OWNING A PERSIAN

Everything about the Persian is soft and rounded. The coat is about 4 in. (10 cm.) long, longer on the ruff and in some top show cats. It is fine and matts easily, making this a breed that demands a considerable investment of time in grooming. The body is broad and cobby, carried on short legs. The head is rounded, and the ears have rounded tips. Cats in North America tend to have the shortest noses, and the CFA breed standard calls for forehead, nose, and chin to be in vertical alignment, while in the United Kingdom the GCCF standard calls for a "short, broad nose with a stop."

SILVER TABBY This blotched or classic tabby is the traditional tabby pattern of the Persian, with others only being allowed much later. Cats with silvered coats have green eyes.

Birman

ORIGIN France or Burma, now Myanmar (1920s)

SYNONYM Sacred Cat of Burma

WEIGHT 10–18 lb. (4.5–8 kg.)

BUILD 🐈

TEMPERAMENT 🐈

COAT CARE 🖌🖌🖌

COLORS All colors in self and tortie; all tabby patterns; always in pointed pattern with white mittens

The first pointed longhair breed, the Birman is a silky, elegant cat with an angelic expression, and it has a religious history to match. Or has it? From its very first appearance, suspicion has been attached to the official version of its origins, with many suspecting that French creative flair lies behind those glamourpuss looks.

BLUE POINT

CARAMEL POINT

CHOCOLATE POINT

BLUE TABBY POINT

BREED LEGEND

The legend of the Birman starts in Burma (now Myanmar), in a temple to Tsun Kyan-Kse, a goddess of the Khmer people who presided over the passage of souls. The temple held a magnificent golden statue of her with sapphires for eyes. Here one hundred pure white cats lived; when a priest died, his soul entered the body of such a sacred animal to be reborn when it died. During an attack on the temple, the head priest, Mun-Ha lay dying. One particular golden-eyed cat, named Sinh, who was the companion of the head priest, leapt onto him, his eyes fixed on the statue of the goddess. His coat took on the golden tones of the statue and the brown shades of the earth, except where his feet touched the head of Mun-Ha, and his eyes became sapphire blue, reflecting those of the goddess.

So far, so poetic. But how did the breed get from the mountains of Burma to the show halls of Europe? Amid rumors of temple cats being given to Westerners as a reward, or even stolen, all that is certain is that a breed by the name of Sacre de Birmanie, the Sacred Cat of Burma, was registered in France in 1925. Sceptics point out that this is just when breeders in Europe were

SEAL POINT This is the original color of the Birman, but as the Siamese arrived carrying the genes blue and possibly chocolate, such genes probably also lay in the Birman.

making the first crosses of Persians with Siamese to create the forerunners of the Colourpoint or Himalayan Persians.

Whatever its origins, the breed almost died out in World War II, necessitating outcrossing to appropriate breeds. The revived breed was accepted on both sides of the Atlantic during the 1960s; today it is in the top ten breeds in the United Kingdom and United States. The Birman and its legend are well established around the world, and unlikely to fade away again.

OWNING A BIRMAN

The Birman requires a little devotion. The long, soft coat needs regular care to keep it sleek and tangle-free. The breed is fairly healthy, with no major hereditary disorders.

In personality, this dedicated companion is described as quiet but sociable. It is said to prefer not to be the only pet in the home—a hundred cats may be too many for most people, but do consider two.

LILAC POINT This recessive of chocolate was among the four "traditional" colors that were the only ones accepted by CFA until relatively recently.

RED POINT This color does not seem to have been known in the breed before World War II, but outcrosses due to lack of stock brought it in during the 1950s.

Ragdoll

ORIGIN United States (1960s)

SYNONYM None

WEIGHT 10–20 lb. (4.5–9 kg.)

BUILD 🐈

TEMPERAMENT 🐈

COAT CARE 🪮

COLORS All colors except cinnamon and fawn in self and tortie; all tabby patterns; always in pointed pattern and either mitted or bicolor

It's hard to believe that such a charming looking cat as this could have been at the center of decades of controversy and feuding. But myths, outrageous claims, and divisions are all elements in the story of the Ragdoll and its quite extraordinary founding breeder.

SEAL POINT	BLUE POINT	LILAC POINT	CHOCOLATE POINT	RED TABBY POINT & WHITE	LILAC TABBY POINT

BREED ORIGINS

Genetically, the breed began when Ann Baker, a Californian breeder of Persians, began selecting kittens out of Josephine, a white, non-pedigree, longhair cat who ran free in her neighborhood. These kittens were by a number of nonpedigree sires, mostly unknown, but some of Burmese and Birman type. Josephine was mated to two of her sons. Among the offspring of these matings were two females: All Ragdolls descended from these two males and two females.

POINTED AND MITTED One of the founder males, Daddy Warbucks, was a mitted Birman-type cat, and some registries resisted the breed in part because of this "lookalike" trait.

Ann Baker began registering Ragdolls in 1965, and started selling them. She began working with other breeders, but kept control over all breeding decisions. In 1971, she founded her own registry, the International Ragdoll Cat Association (IRCA), and trademarked the breed

to entitle her to demand royalties from other breeders for using it.

Breeders who were chafing under Ann Baker's restrictive regime started another association, the Ragdoll Fanciers' Club International (RFCI). Chief among them were Denny and Laura Dayton. The efforts of the

Daytons and others saw the breed achieve some recognition. CFA remained resolutely opposed to the breed, but by the end of the decade, it was established within the newly formed TICA. Now shown by all major registries, this popular breed sits in the top ten cats on both sides of the Atlantic.

OWNING A RAGDOLL

Ann Baker made five claims for the Ragdoll (and many outlandish ones surrounding its origins): That they are relatively large, have almost magically nonmatting fur, lack the skills and instincts for self-preservation, go limp when you hold them, and are less sensitive to pain than other cats. So which of these hold any truth? They are large, imposing cats, but not outrageously so. Their fur lacks a dense undercoat and is less prone to matting than the coat of a Persian, but still requires

grooming. As for the supposed fearlessness, Ragdolls are no more foolhardy than any other breed. They do tend to relax when picked up to a greater degree than other breeds. The most irresponsible claim, that they do not feel pain like other cats, is utterly false.

SEAL BICOLOR Seal is still the most commonly found color of Ragdoll.

RagaMuffin

By the mid-1990s, some breeders who had been working with Ann Baker were seeking to set up on their own and work within major registries, just as in the 1970s. And so, in 1994, they broke away and petitioned for recognition of their cats in several associations. Because of the trademark held by Ann Baker on the name Ragdoll, these breeders chose the name RagaMuffin for their breakaway breed. Unsurprisingly, the easygoing personality and easycare coat of this breed are essentially the same as those of the Ragdoll.

Maine Coon

ORIGIN United States (1800s)

SYNONYM American Longhair, Maine Cat, Maine Shag

WEIGHT 9–22 lb. (4–10 kg.)

BUILD

TEMPERAMENT

COAT CARE

COLORS Western colors in self, tortie, bicolor, solid, smoke, and shaded; classic and mackerel tabby patterns

This is the first, most famous, and still most popular national breed of the United States. It is the gentle giant of the cat world, renowned for its size, its sociable nature, and its reputation for enjoying a swim. Its history is not one long success story, however: The Maine Coon made perhaps the greatest comeback in feline history.

BLACK SELF

BLUE SELF (LONG)

BLUE & WHITE

BROWN STRIPED TABBY

SILVER TABBY

BROWN TABBY & WHITE

BREED ORIGINS

The early origins of the Maine Coon are the subject of many colorful legends. It was suggested that it was the hybrid offspring of domestic cats and the bobcat, or even of cats interbreeding with raccoons. One popular tale holds that this longhair is descended from ancestral Norwegian Forest Cats brought over to North America by ancient Vikings. Another gives it classier ancestors: The royal pets of Marie Antoinette. Perhaps the most charming, but least likely, tale involves a sea captain named Coon whose longhaired cats left progeny in every port. In truth, the Maine

Coon probably descended from cats that came in ships with successive groups of settlers. Somewhere in this founder population was the longhaired gene for a thick coat that gave the cats a survival advantage in the harsh continental winters. A large size also made them less attractive as prey for local wildlife, and enabled them as hunters to tackle larger animals such as hares.

The first breed shows brought success for the Maine Coon, but in the early 20th century more exotic breeds, such as the Persian, held sway. The Maine Coon was starting to slip into a 40-year period of obscurity. In the early 1950s, a club was formed to revive the breed. Relentless showing and publicity brought measurable success by the early 1960s, with the Maine again

TABBY BICOLORS Originally only cats of tabby pattern were called coon cats. Tufted ears, like a bobcat, are part of the Maine "look."

being bred to a written standard. Show successes eventually followed, and by the end of the millennium, the breed was second only to the Persian in popularity.

Unlike many other American breeds, the Maine Coon was a highly successful export. It was recognized by both FIFé and the GCCF; in the United Kingdom it started from scratch in the 1980s to sit comfortably in the top ten breeds within a decade.

OWNING A MAINE COON

Although it is longhaired, the Maine Coon does not require painstaking grooming. It has a shaggy look (hence the alternative name of Maine Shag) and needs piecemeal attention to trouble spots rather than allover, everyday grooming. However, there is an inherited tendency to heart trouble.

Maines are described by their owners as gentle, loyal, and reliably good with children and other pets. They are sociable but not intrusive, and active but laid back.

RED TABBY Only the blotched and striped tabby patterns are allowed in the Maine Coon. This is in keeping with its origins among early exports from Europe.

CREAM TABBY AND WHITE Bicolor cats must have white on the bib, the belly, and all four paws. The cream tabby has buff markings on a very pale cream ground.

Norwegian Forest Cat

ORIGIN Norway (1930s)

SYNONYM Skaukatt, Norsk Skogkatt, Wegie

WEIGHT 7–20 lb. (3–9 kg.)

BUILD

TEMPERAMENT

COAT CARE

COLORS Western colors in self, tortie, bicolor, solid, smoke, shaded, and tipped; blotched, striped, and spotted tabby patterns

Scandinavia's "little lynx" is a self-contained, self-reliant, hardy longhair, equally comfortable in the snowy forests of its homeland or more moderate climes abroad. Popular across Europe and in North America, it is seen by its fans as the cat sacred to the Norse goddess Freya, powerful enough to draw her chariot.

BLUE SELF (LONG)	RED SELF	RED & WHITE	BROWN CLASSIC TABBY	SILVER STRIPED TABBY	BLACK SMOKE

BREED ORIGINS

It is known from archaeological evidence that the domestic cat was well established in Scandinavia before 1000AD. It may well be that the longhaired mutation, thought to have arisen somewhere in the near East, arrived in Scandinavia well before it was imported into western Europe in the ancestors of the Persian.

The ancestors of today's breed had a distinct advantage over smaller, shorthaired arrivals in the country. Their long, glossy, water repellent coat is a perfect protection from the harsh Scandinavian winters, and their muscular, imposing build makes them both unattractive prey and fearsome predators. Over time, long hair became a more common trait in Scandinavian farm and household cats.

In the late 1930s, examples of the Skaukatt or Norsk Skogkatt (literally Norwegian forest cat) were shown to great acclaim in Germany. A group of breeders made efforts to preserve the type that had evolved, before it faded into the general feline population. World War II interrupted these efforts, however, as it did for many breeds across Europe, and in the 1950s, the task was taken up again by breeders who eventually established a formal breed club in 1975. Two of these breeders, Egil and Else Nyland, bred the legendary Pan's Truls. This magnificent male is regarded as the epitome of the breed, and served as the model for the written breed standard. This was adopted by FIFé, and the Norwegian Forest Cat was also designated the official cat of Norway by King Olaf.

Two years after full recognition in Europe, Norwegians reached the United States, where they were soon

SILVER TORTIE TABBY AND WHITE The face is an equilateral triangle, with large, tufted ears, and almond-shaped eyes. The body is substantial, with the hind legs longer than the front, and large feet turned out at the toe.

BLACK SELF Self colors are not seen as often as tabbies and bicolors. FIFé and the GCCF, unlike North American registries, allocate no points for color or pattern.

OWNING A WEGIE

The coat is double, with a woolly, insulating undercoat and long, glossy, water-repellent topcoat. It is given considerable importance in most breed standards, with the word "coarse" being used of the topcoat. The Norwegian is only allowed in the traditional Western colors, although a new mutation that produces Oriental-seeming colors that change markedly as the cat matures is causing a rewrite of standards in some registries.

The heavy coat is a triumph of functional design, and needs a bit of help every few days to look its best, not a full-body groom every day. However, daily brushing is needed during the annual molts.

The Norwegian is an enterprising breed that will rise to most situations: Children, visitors, and other pets will not daunt it. It is a cool, calm, and collected breed, not a lap cat, intelligently cautious but perfectly sociable with those that it trusts.

nicknamed Wegies. They were recognized by TICA first, in the 1980s, then CFA and other associations. In the United Kingdom, the GCCF began registering cats in the 1980s; from a very small start the Norwegian rose to just outside the top ten breeds within 20 years.

BLUE (LEFT) AND CREAM (RIGHT) The gene for blue is distributed across the feline world. The gene for red and cream is most common at the Nile delta, on the Scottish isles, and in Scandinavia.

Siberian

ORIGIN Russia (1980s)

SYNONYM Neva Masquerade

WEIGHT 10–20 lb. (4.5–9 kg.)

BUILD 🐈

TEMPERAMENT 🐈

COAT CARE ✂✂

COLORS Western (and Eastern in TICA) colors in self, tortie, bicolor, solid, smoke, shaded, and tipped; all tabby patterns; pointed pattern in CFA and TICA

For most of the 20th century, no new cat breeds came out of Russia, where Communist ideology scorned breeding. With the end of the Soviet era, not only people and ideas but animal breeds of all sorts began to move. The West gained the Siberian and Kurilean, and Russia has a fledgling cat fancy.

WHITE	BLUE SELF (LONG)	BLUE & WHITE	CREAM STRIPED TABBY	SILVER SHADED	SEAL TABBY POINT

BREED ORIGINS

Finding the truth amid Siberian myths is like catching smoke. Anecdotal accounts have cats trekking to Siberia with Russian settlers, or living, like so many romanticized breeds, in monasteries. Their descendants made the long return trip to Moscow and Leningrad, where the new cat clubs could, apparently, distinguish them from other nonpedigree longhairs on sale for much less in the markets. In truth, the Siberian may not be Siberian at all, but it is certainly a Russian cat.

In 1990, three were shipped by a Russian breed club to Elizabeth Terrell, a breeder in the United States, and 15 were imported by David Boehm, who visited Leningrad and Moscow to buy cats at a show and in markets. It is recognized in North America, and by FIFé in Europe, but not yet by the GCCF.

OWNING A SIBERIAN

First, is the Siberian hypoallergenic? Breeders say test results for Fel D1 in saliva showed less of the protein in Siberians, but scientists say the results were misinterpreted, and this breed is not the long sought hypoallergenic cat.

The Siberian has much the same appeal as the Maine Coon and the Norwegian Forest Cat. It is usually seen in the same naturally Western colors: Pointed cats, sometimes called Neva Masquerades, are rarely seen. The original importer is quoted as saying that "we've never found anything they're afraid of" and that they are "the most affectionate things I've ever seen."

PROVING GROUND The long, weatherproof coats and take on all comers bravado of the Siberian are said to have been fostered by the extreme conditions of the taiga or boreal forest.

SIBERIAN COAT The Siberian is described as possessing a triple coat, adults having a particularly tight, dense undercoat beneath the longer layers.

Balinese (including Javanese)

ORIGIN United States (1950s)

SYNONYM Javanese

WEIGHT 6–11 lb. (2.5–5 kg.)

BUILD

TEMPERAMENT

COAT CARE

COLORS All colors in self and tortie; all tabby patterns; always in pointed pattern

This breed—or these breeds, depending on your registry—arrived late on the scene. By the time they were developed, the pointing gene was already available in two longhaired breeds, both of them at the chunky and cuddly end of the scale. The Balinese finally presented a pointed, longhaired cat for those who prefer svelte.

LILAC POINT   CREAM POINT   CHOCOLATE POINT   FAWN POINT   SEAL TABBY POINT   RED TABBY POINT & WHITE

RED TABBY OR LYNX POINT This is a Balinese in most registries, but a Javanese in CFA. The Javanese breed is less popular than the Balinese.

BREED ORIGINS

The longhaired gene may have been present in the Siamese when the cats first arrived from their Oriental home, or it may have appeared through an accidental or deliberate outcrossing early in its history as a breed. In the years following World War II, Marion Dorsey in California started to breed and show "Longhaired Siamese" and they were recognized in American registries by 1961. Siamese breeders objected to the name, and it was changed to Balinese, inspired by the sinuous, elegant dancers of the island's temples. The breed spread from North America in the 1970s, and is recognized by all major registries around the world today.

There is some division over colors between registries. TICA and registries in Europe and elsewhere recognize both eumelanistic and pheomelanistic colors, as well as

BLUE POINT Dilute colors are more liable to be confused than dense ones. Blue points should be cool—impossible to mistake for the warmer lilac points.

tabby patterns. But CFA accepts only four colors in the Balinese—seal, blue, chocolate, and lilac—and classifies all other colors and patterns in a separate offshoot called Javanese.

OWNING A BALINESE

The silky coat is fairly low maintenance, and when it is shed in summer, cats can appear shorthaired apart from their plumelike tail. They are long lived cats, and more robust than their delicate build suggests.

Like all the Oriental breeds, it has a loud voice which it will use to remind you that it needs your attention and admiration. The Balinese is an active and inquisitive breed, and will get everywhere.

Oriental Longhair

ORIGIN United Kingdom and United States (1970s on)

SYNONYM Angora, Javanese, Mandarin

WEIGHT 10–13 lb. (4.5–6 kg.)

BUILD

TEMPERAMENT

COAT CARE

COLORS All colors in self, tortie, bicolor, solid, smoke, shaded, and tipped; all tabby patterns

This is the last of the quartet of Oriental breeds that first came to the West in the eye-catching pattern of the Siamese. Solid colors were barred, becoming the Oriental Shorthair, but the longhair gene eventually gave us both the Balinese and this elegant breed.

BLACK SELF	WHITE	LILAC SELF	RED TICKED TABBY	BLACK SMOKE	BLUE TORTIE TABBY & WHITE

BREED ORIGINS

The Oriental Longhair has different origins on either side of the Atlantic. In the United Kingdom, breeder Maureen Silson mated a Siamese with an Abyssinian, hoping to get a ticked tabby point Siamese. Unexpectedly the kittens included longhairs. The longhairs began to appear at shows in the 1970s, but under the name Angora: They were seen as a recreation of the longhairs that had died out in Europe at the end of the 19th century, and the Turkish Angora had not yet reached British shores. In Europe the new breed was recognized as the Javanese, to avoid confusion with the Turkish cats; this name has now changed in FIFé, but remains in use in New Zealand. Progress was slow: Mating back to Siamese and

WHITE The United Kingdom has a longhaired equivalent of the Foreign White with its Siamese blue eyes and avoidance of deafness problems.

Oriental Shorthairs meant many short-haired and pointed kittens. Angoras only achieved full Championship status in 2003, and at this point were officially renamed Oriental Longhairs.

In the United States, the breed had a later start, in 1985. Here the parents were an Oriental Shorthair and a Balinese at Sheryl Ann Boyle's Sholine Cattery. An accidental mating produced solid and pointed longhair and shorthair kittens. Boyle developed the solid longhairs as a breed, named Oriental Longhair, and it was rapidly

CINNAMON (LEFT) AND BLUE TABBY (RIGHT) The first important cat of the breed in the United Kingdom was a cinnamon. All variants of tabby patterns are shown.

ALL ORIENTALS Pointed members of the Oriental groups are still allowed as outcross breeds. A litter of solid kittens like this is what all breeders want, but occasional pointed offspring will turn up.

recognized by major registries across North America and Europe, except for the GCCF.

In these four linked breeds—Oriental Longhair, Oriental Shorthair, Balinese, and Siamese—the solid colors will produce pointed variants and the shorthairs will produce longhairs; the status of these for showing vary. TICA has one root standard for all, and in 1995 CFA merged the Oriental Shorthair and Longhair into one breed with two coat lengths, which upset breeders who feared that the longhair gene could subtly affect the quality of the shorthair coat.

OWNING AN ORIENTAL LONGHAIR

The coat of the Oriental Longhair is often not that long, especially in summer, a warm climate, or cats kept permanently indoors in warm homes; these may look like shorthairs but for a plumed tail. The fineness of the sleek coat makes it one of the easiest longhairs to care for.

Like all its Oriental sibling breeds, this is an active and athletic cat that likes to do rather than see things. It is also gregarious to the point of absurdity, and can gossip for hours.

BLUE SELF The blue of the Oriental Longhair should be free from any trace of the silver tipping that is prized in some other breeds.

Tiffanie

ORIGIN United Kingdom (1970s)
SYNONYM Longhair Burmilla
WEIGHT 8–14 lb. (3.5–6.5 kg.)
BUILD
TEMPERAMENT
COAT CARE
COLORS All colors in self, tortie, and shaded; all tabby patterns; sepia pattern

This gorgeous cat is of a type that remains unusual in the feline breed spectrum: A longhaired cat of moderately foreign type. While there are a few big, wild, farm-cat type longhairs, even more cute and cuddly fluffy ones, and a choice of slender, slinky Oriental types, the Tiffanie stands almost without competition in its homeland.

RED SELF

LILAC SELF

SILVER TABBY

BLACK TICKED TABBY

BLACK SMOKE

CHINCHILLA

BREED ORIGINS

The Tiffanie is a member of the otherwise shorthaired Asian group and so shares their initial parentage, which was the unplanned alliance of a young chinchilla Persian male and a Burmese female in 1981. The Persian obviously contributed his longhaired trait to the offspring, but in the first generation it was masked by the dominant shorthaired trait of their mother. From the second generation of kittens on, fluffy coats appeared, and although disregarded at first, they eventually progressed with the rest of the Asian group.

The breed reached full Championship status a little later than the shorthaired members of the group, just after the turn of the millennium. It is still only recognized in the United Kingdom. In Europe, FIFé recognized only the Asian shaded, under its original name of Burmilla. There is also an Australian Tiffanie, first recognized in 1999. This was created out of longhaired kittens that turned up in litters from Asian cats; ultimately, it shares the same origins as the British breed, but its immediate parents are different, and it remains to be seen how similar these two Tiffanies on opposite sides of the globe will prove to be.

In North America, there has always been a problem of confusion between this cat and another longhaired breed that was at first called the Tiffany. This chocolate-colored cat, often described as a longhaired Burmese although its origins were in fact unknown, was later renamed the Chantilly/Tiffany, but to no avail. Although

LILAC SMOKE In the Australian Tiffanie, which is officially listed by the Australian Cat Federation as the longhaired Burmilla, shades of lilac are the rarest of the colors seen.

recognized by the Canadian Cat Association, it has faded into obscurity.

OWNING A TIFFANIE

For Brits who want an elegant but not supermodel longhair, this is a good choice; elsewhere, the Turkish Angora provides similar grace. The coat needs grooming a few times a week, more during molting. Polycystic kidney disease came into the breed from the Persian heritage, but a test allows this to be detected and eliminated from breeding lines.

In personality, the Tiffanie is a reasonable medium between the extrovert Burmese and the placid Persian, with an outgoing but easygoing nature.

BLUE SMOKE The most common coats, even within the broad range recognized in the United Kingdom, are smokes, shaded, which are heavily mantled with color, and tipped.

RED SHADED SILVER The red colors were developed rather later in the Asian group than the eumelanistic shades, and are judged separately in FIFé and Australian registries.

CHOCOLATE SHADED SILVER Solid, sepia, and tabby patterned Tiffanies are accepted in the United Kingdom, reflecting the whole Asian coat spectrum.

Turkish Van

ORIGIN Turkey (before 1700s)
SYNONYM Turkish swimming cat; Vankedisi
WEIGHT 7–19 lb. (3–8.5 kg.)
BUILD 🐈
TEMPERAMENT 🐈
COAT CARE 🪮
COLORS Western colors in self and tortie; all tabby patterns; always van pattern bicolor; all-white cats known as Vankedisi in GCCF

One of two breeds to come out of Turkey, this cat looks a big softie. It has a sweet, rounded face; big eyes, sometimes in baby blue; and a soft, long coat that constantly shifts and flows as it moves. But it is a natural breed from a harsh, rugged terrain, and although exotic, it is no lap cat.

WHITE   BLACK & WHITE   BLUE & WHITE   TORTIE TABBY   BLUE TORTIE &
                                             & WHITE   WHITE

CREAM AND WHITE The ideal Van is completely white on the body with a colored tail and head markings. One or more markings are allowed on the body, and some white on the tail.

BREED ORIGINS

The Turkish Van is a naturally distilled breed, originating around Lake Van in the mountains of eastern Turkey, where it can still be found breeding true without human intervention. The region is relatively isolated, exactly the circumstances that favor the development of a distinctive local type.

The bicolor pattern, predominantly white with isolated color on the head and tail, is generally known in the cat fancy as the van pattern, after this breed. Although claims that cats of this pattern appear in Hittite art may be pushing the bounds of possibility back too far, it can be seen in old works of art from the near East, both local and painted by foreigners who clearly saw it as characteristic of the place. Later studies have confirmed this: The pattern is found in a relatively high percentage of cats here, but is rare elsewhere in the world.

In 1955, two British women visiting Turkey, Laura Lushington and Sonia Halliday, brought some of the cats home with them. Laura's kittens endured a car tour and camping en route, showing them to be fairly adaptable creatures. They bred true, confirming they were a true natural variety, not a mere coincidence.

Lushington worked for recognition of the cats in the United Kingdom, where they became known at first as Turkish cats. The Turkish Angora not being a recognized breed in the country, this name seemed to make perfect sense. The breed arrived on the shores of the United States in 1982, and had Championship showing status in TICA and CFA by 1994. It remains rare in both North America and Europe, however, with

TORTIE AND WHITE Unusually, the eumelanistic colors were recognized in this breed after the pheomelanistic. The markings above the tail are known as thumbprints.

only a hundred cats registered each year. Their numbers have also diminished in recent years in their homeland but, like the Turkish Angora, they have government protection and are bred in Ankhara zoo. In the United Kingdom, the GCCF has begun the process of recognizing an all-white strain of the cat under the name Vankedisi; the name Van Kedi has also been applied to the bicolor Van.

OWNING A TURKISH VAN

Bred by nature in an uncompromising environment, these are resourceful, intelligent, and fairly independent cats. They are gregarious, but prefer joint activities to lounging around simply purring, and have seemingly unlimited energy. The original breeder, Laura Lushington, noted that "their outstanding characteristic is their liking for water … they not only dabble in water and play with it, but have been known to enter ponds and even horse-troughs for a swim."

AUBURN AND WHITE
Auburn is the breed name for red, and this is the "classic" Van color and pattern. The markings on the head should be symmetrical.

Turkish Angora

ORIGIN Turkey (before 1700s)
SYNONYM None
WEIGHT 6–11 lb. (2.5–5 kg.)
BUILD
TEMPERAMENT
COAT CARE
COLORS Western colors in self, tortie, bicolor, smoke, and shaded; blotched and striped tabby patterns

Possibly the oldest longhaired breed in the world, the Angora found fame in Europe, nearly went extinct, was rescued by a zoo and the government, found a new life in the United States, and spread back to Europe and beyond. At the end of this rocky ride, it still closely resembles the cats depicted in old artworks.

 BLACK SELF
 BLUE SELF
 RED SELF
 BROWN CLASSIC TABBY
 SILVER TABBY
CHINCHILLA

BREED ORIGINS

The mutation for long hair is generally thought to have arisen many centuries ago in central Asia and spread outward. The first recorded imports into Europe, in the 17th century, came from Persia to Italy with Pietro della Valle, and from Turkey (and more particularly, Angora, now Ankhara) to France with Nicolas-Claude Fabri de Pieresc; hence the designation of the first two longhaired breeds. In the late 19th century, it was the Persian that took off and passed on the longhair trait to most of the other longhaired breeds created in the 20th century. The Angora languished in obscurity, becoming virtually extinct beyond and even within its homeland.

Fortunately, there was a small breeding population kept in the zoo at Ankhara. Starting in 1917, the zoo undertook a concerted breeding scheme to save the cats. As with all zoo conservation

CREAM AND WHITE Bicolors and red shades are common in Turkey. The inverted V on the face is also a classic marking and noted as desirable in the CFA standard.

efforts, the breedings were carefully controlled and recorded, with great care taken to establish as broad a genetic base as possible, and the zoo staff were very reluctant to part with any cats.

Finally, in 1962, Walter and Liesa Fallon Grant managed to wrest a breeding pair of unrelated cats from the Ankhara zoo and started a breeding line in the United States. Other breeders were also beginning to import these elegant, silky cats and by the 1970s the breed was recognized by CFA in a range of colors and patterns. Today, the Turkish Angora hovers somewhere

TORTOISESHELL SMOKE Smokes were recorded in 19th-century writings. The shimmer of the silver undercoat is seen at its best in winter when the coat is longest.

in the middle of the popularity rankings published each year by CFA.

In Europe, the breed is recognized by FIFé, with a good number of breeders in several countries. In the United Kingdom, the GCCF has not yet recognized it.

OWNING A TURKISH ANGORA

Harrison Weir described these cats in his book *Our Cats* in 1889: "The best are … a pure white with blue eyes, being thought the perfection of cats … and its hearing by no means defective." He mentions other colors including the black, "which should have orange eyes, as should the slate colors and the blues." Today all these are once more recognized; only colors that hint at an outcross to Oriental breeds are forbidden.

The silky, semilong coat has no undercoat and lies smooth against the body, shimmering with every movement. The body is long and lithe, but muscular. The head is a moderate wedge of smooth lines, tapering evenly into a fairly narrow muzzle. Large ears give the breed a characteristically alert, interested look.

Turkish Angoras are lively, intelligent, active, and athletic; it is unclear whether their minds or their bodies work faster, but either one will prove an enjoyable challenge to keep up with.

CREAM TABBY As the dilute form of red, this shade is common in the Angora's homeland. In pedigree cats, the colors must be warm and rich, never sandy.

BLUE-CREAM The breed standards allow for the colors of torties and blue torties to be either patchy or softly and evenly intermingled across the cat's body.

Somali

ORIGIN North America (1960s)

SYNONYM Longhaired Abyssinian

WEIGHT 8–12 lb. (3.5–5.5 kg.)

BUILD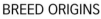

TEMPERAMENT

COAT CARE

COLORS All colors in self, tortie, and shaded (brown, blue, cinnamon, and fawn only in CFA); always in ticked tabby pattern

Even harmless recessive genes sometimes seem like a dirty secret. The Russian Shorthair, Siamese, and Abyssinian all carried long hair, but it took decades for breeders to move to developing their attractive, fluffy kittens. They all did eventually, and the Somali is one of the happy results.

BROWN TICKED TABBY

BLUE TICKED TABBY

RED TICKED TABBY

BREED ORIGINS

It is not clear when the longhaired gene came into the Abyssinian breed, or whether it was present from the start; given the way that recessive genes can hide for many generations, it is quite possible that the very first cats carried it.

SORREL Most of the thick coat that makes a Somali look so magnificent in winter is shed in spring. Sorrel is the breed name for cinnamon.

For a long time, the slightly fuzzy kittens that turned up in litters were neutered and passed on as pets, and nobody talked about them—breeders can be cagey about recessive variants that seem to undermine the "purity" of a breed if not properly understood.

One particular line of Abys, from British breeder Jean Robertson, seemed to consistently produce these variants. In the 1960s, Ken

Any color you like

The colors that are allowed in the Somali vary greatly internationally. CFA is most restrictive in colors, allowing only ruddy (brown tabby), red (cinnamon), and their dilutes blue and fawn, and no silvers. FIFé follows the same palette of four colors, and TICA recognizes only the eumelanistic colors, so there are no reds, creams, or any torties, but both of these registries do allow silver cats. The GCCF in the United Kingdom, often quite a traditional registry, has the widest range, showing all colors in both solid and silver.

BLUE SILVER The pure white undercoats give silver Somalis quite a different, more dramatic effect. Most of the coat appears to have a veil of color drawn over it.

McGill in Canada began breeding from these lines. Canadian breeder Don Richings then used McGill's cats and began working with American breeder Mary Mague, who was also developing the longhairs and calling them Somalis. By the late 1970s, the new breed was accepted in North American registries. In the 1980s, they were exported to Europe and beyond, and by the early 1990s, the breed was accepted by registries internationally.

OWNING A SOMALI

The ticking, combined with the tufted ears, luxuriant ruff, bottlebrush thickness of tail, and generally wild appearance of Somalis, has earned them the nickname of "fox cats." In their general build and appearance, they resemble their Abyssinian parents, muscular and athletic with a slightly arched back that gives them the look of a cat about to spring at any moment.

The longer coat can accommodate more bands of ticking, with up to 12 light and dark alternating bands on each hair. This gives a luminous depth and shimmer to the coat in a fully developed adult—the coat can take years to mature.

The Somali is a fairly easycare cat, although it is prone to the same inherited problems as its Aby ancestors. It is intelligent, active, and interested in all that goes on around it. Although more gregarious than older European breeds, it does not tend to try and join in with all your activities like Oriental types. If you have two of these cats, they will occupy themselves for much of the time, although you may find yourself checking up on exactly what they are doing, because their curiosity will lead them into strange places.

RUDDY OR USUAL Just as in the Aby, this coat has idiosyncratic names, being called usual in the United Kingdom and ruddy in North America.

Cornish Rex (UK)

ORIGIN United Kingdom (1950s)

SYNONYM None

WEIGHT 6–10 lb. (2.5–4.5 kg.)

BUILD 🐈

TEMPERAMENT 🐆

COAT CARE 🪥

COLORS All colors in all shades and all patterns

There have been earlier historical reports of cats with bristly or wavy hair, but the Cornish was the first such cat to be turned into a successful breed. Its velvety coat and elegant looks are well established now, but the breed had a rocky start in life when the demand for novelty was less pronounced than it is today.

BLUE & WHITE

CREAM STRIPED TABBY

BLUE TABBY & WHITE

BLUE TORTIE TABBY & WHITE

BLUE TABBY POINT

BREED ORIGINS

The first cat known with the mutation appeared in a litter born to a tortie and white female owned by Nina Ennismore of Bodmin in Cornwall. Test breedings showed the mutation to be recessive. Breeder Brian Sterling-Webb continued the work in the 1950s, but many feared that the fledgling breed was unsustainable. Outbreeding avoided a dangerously small gene pool, but led away from the original Oriental look. By 1967, the Cornish Rex was finally recognized by the GCCF. Several breeds are still approved as outcrosses.

OWNING A CORNISH REX

While a normal, straight coat contains guard, awn, and down hairs, the Cornish coat lacks guard hairs, so feels softer. Because of the minimal coat, these are easycare cats, but they are not the best cold-weather cats.

The look is distinctly foreign, with a wedge-shaped head and mussel-shell ears. The body is slender, of medium length, and carried high on long legs, but is hard and muscular.

This high energy, playful, and adventurous breed is almost always on the move, and likes to climb as much as it likes to run around. Cornish Rexes have earned the nickname "Velcro cats" for their tendency to be found attached to their owners.

CREAM Some accounts hold that the founder male Kallibunker was a cream, others that he was a red. Given his non-pedigree background, either is possible—a very cool red or warm cream might look similar.

Cornish Rex (US)

ORIGIN United Kingdom (1950s) and United States

SYNONYM None

WEIGHT 6–9 lb. (2.5–4 kg.)

BUILD 🐈

TEMPERAMENT 🐈

COAT CARE 🪥

COLORS All colors in all shades and all patterns

The Cornish Rex was developed in parallel in its native home, the United Kingdom, and in North America. Although all originally descended from the same mutation, the two strains developed in slightly different ways from the start, and today the looks are quite distinctly different.

BLACK SELF   BLUE & WHITE   BROWN CLASSIC TABBY   RED STRIPED TABBY   TORTIE TABBY   LILAC POINT

BREED ORIGINS

In 1957, a Californian breeder, Frances Blancheri, imported a son of Kallibunker, Pendennis Castle, and a daughter of another early father, Poldhu, Lamorna Cove, who had been bred to her sire before she was exported. Pendennis Castle had no offspring, but Lamorna Cove gave birth to four kittens, marking the start of the breed in the United States.

When breeders tried to import more of the cats, there were none to be had, and so outcrosses were made to Siamese, American Shorthairs, Burmese, and Havana Browns, starting a drift between the two types.

A rexed female who turned up in a California animal shelter proved to have the same mutation and was taken into the line; whether she had come from it or was a separate mutation is not known. Also, the German Rex arrived in the United States in 1961 and was judged in one class with the Cornish. The highest-ranked Rex ever was Katzenreich's Bianka; as the name implies,

Katzenreich bred German Rexes. The German Rex eventually merged into the Cornish and was forgotten. In 1962, CFA recognized Cornish Rexes and within two years they had full Championship status.

The Cornish remains popular in its adopted home. In fact, hovering a little outside the top ten breeds, it is more popular than it is in the United Kingdom.

CREAM AND WHITE The body type of the American cat is lean and racy, with an arched spine. The chest is deep, but then slims into a whippet-like, tucked-up tummy.

OWNING A CORNISH REX

The build of the Cornish Rexes bred in the United States is more whippetlike and the coat more obviously waved than in their British counterparts. The American Cornish also differs from the British type in its head shape. Where it does not differ is in its appealingly lively, inquisitive, and gregarious personality.

TORTOISESHELL Standards call for a Roman nose, and the "break" at the whisker pads is pronounced; the whole look is more chiseled than the British type.

Devon Rex

ORIGIN United Kingdom (1960s)

SYNONYM None

WEIGHT 6–9 lb. (2.5–4 kg.)

BUILD 🐈

TEMPERAMENT 🐈

COAT CARE 🪮

COLORS All colors in all shades and all patterns

Like so many modern breeds distinguished by a single striking feature, the Devon Rex mutation was first seen in a stray. Of course, mutations occur within breeds too, but they often have a hard time getting accepted. This breed, with its extraordinary elfin looks, had no such problems, and is a popular breed in many countries.

BLUE SELF	RED SELF	SILVER STRIPED TABBY	TORTIE & WHITE	RED POINT	CREAM POINT

BREED ORIGINS

In the 1950s, a curly-coated tomcat was active around Buckfastleigh in the west of England; in fact, cats of this type, locally called the "Buckfast Blue," had been reported around Buckfast Abbey for some time. In 1960, a feral tortoiseshell and white female gave birth to a litter in the garden of Beryl Cox; the litter included a curly-coated kitten, which Cox adopted and named Kirlee.

That year, a newspaper article was published celebrating ten years of the Cornish Rex, with a picture of what was claimed to be the only curly-coated kitten in the country. Miss Cox contacted the newspaper to tell them about her kitten, and was put in touch with Cornish Rex breeder Brian Sterling-Webb. They arranged for Kirlee to be sent to Cornwall to be part of the breeding program. However, when Kirlee was bred to several Cornish Rex females, the kittens were all straight-coated. Kirlee was recognized as a different rex mutation, called Gene II.

One breeder, Mrs P. Hughes, had kept a straight coated female, named Broughton Golden Rain, from one of the crossed litters. When she was bred back to Kirlee, she produced two straight-coated kittens and one curly female. This first curly-coated offspring of Kirlee showed the Devon Rex gene to be a simple recessive.

By 1967, the breed was recognized by the GCCF, and over the next decade it spread around the world. In 1968, breeder Marion White and her daughter Anita imported two cats to Texas after seeing them while in the United Kingdom, and in 1969, another Texas breeder, Shirley Lambert, imported a pair. These two

CREAM TABBY POINT There have been pointed Devons, sometimes called si-rexes, since the early days; two of the first cats imported into the United States were seal points.

breeders were the spearhead of interest that spread to other states and to Canada through the 1970s.

But in North America, the Devon was hampered by CFA rules. They were judged simply as rexed cats, against a standard drawn up for the Cornish Rex, which had arrived first. Unwilling to lose the distinctive looks of the Devon by breeding to another cat's standard, breeders looked elsewhere, and the breed was recognized and shown in ACFA and later TICA instead. In 1979, CFA had a change of heart, and the Devon was recognized as a breed in its own right, reaching Championship status by 1983.

OWNING A DEVON

The Devon has guard, awn, and down hairs. Although the guard hairs are sparse and short, they give the Devon coat a looser, more open-looking curl than the Cornish Rex. Like the Cornish, this is not a hypoallergenic cat, but it is low maintenance. Early inbreeding resulted in some health problems—

BLUE SELF The original Devon Rex, Kirlee, is variously described as gray, black, or brownish black. He is most likely to have been a blue, like his sire.

luxating patella (slipping kneecaps), coagulopathy, and inherited spasticity —but testing and outcrossing have been and still are used to reduce these.

As for personality, Devons look like mischief makers, and they live up to their looks, but usually only enough to endear them to their owners.

TABBY POINT The pointed pattern can be combined with any other pattern in the Devon Rex, so tabby or lynx points, shaded silver points, and bicolor points are all allowed.

TORTOISESHELL The Devon profile shows a curved forehead and a clear stop before the short muzzle. The breed has a broad chest, widely spaced front legs, and a muscular body.

RED TABBY The Devon "look" favors females or younger cats. This face is too full and heavy for perfection, due to stud jowls that develop in males kept intact for breeding.

Selkirk Rex

ORIGIN United States (1980s)

SYNONYM None

WEIGHT 7–11 lb. (3–5 kg.)

BUILD 🐈

TEMPERAMENT 🐈

COAT CARE ✂️

COLORS All colors in all shades and all patterns

There are fashions in feline breeds. Once, curly-coated cats were oddities to be shunned, an attitude that changed only with better understanding of genetics. The Selkirk is the most recent of the rexed breeds to be developed, and is proving to be healthy and popular: The breed motto might be "never be first, only be best."

BLACK　　WHITE　　BLUE SELF　　BLACK SMOKE　　SEAL POINT　　LILAC POINT

TORTIE SMOKE (LEFT) The ideal smoke should look like a self at rest, showing the undercoat when it moves. In rexed cats, a hint of the undercoat always shows.

BLUE-CREAM (RIGHT) Pest and her mother both wore this blue-cream coat with a little added white.

BREED ORIGINS

In 1987, a dilute tortie kitten with thick, curled hair unlike all her littermates appeared in a litter born at the home of Kitty Brown in Sheridan, Montana. Peggy Vorrhees of the Bozeman Humane Society took the young cat, named her Miss DePesto, and showed her to Jeri Newman, a breeder of Persians in Livingston, Montana, interested in genetics and unusual cats. Miss DePesto, or Pest, went home with Newman to become the mother of a new breed.

It seemed unlikely that Pest was the offspring of another pedigree rexed breed running around mating with local cats. Newman was taken by the thick coat and robust build of the cat, but felt that the head was not a good match. She described Pest as the "world's

BLACK SMOKE AND WHITE The Selkirk face is broad and full-cheeked, with a muzzle wider than it is long and convex in profile, and a rounded head.

breed is accepted in all major North American registries, and is the most successful native rexed breed to date. Overseas, it is not recognized by FIFé, and European breeders show it in TICA. It is accepted by the GCCF and gaining in popularity. It is also a Championship breed in Australia.

OWNING A SELKIRK REX

In head and body, the Selkirk Rex is a cobby cat, similar to the British Shorthair. The build is sturdy, but the legs are longer than the British type.

The underlying coat quality is thick and soft, and feels plush to the touch. Guard, awn, and down hairs are present, showing a random arrangement of loose curls. The underside, flanks, and neck show the most curl, the back the least. There are both shorthaired and longhaired versions, the latter having an even more eye-catching, ringletted coat.

The soft Selkirk coat is much the better for being left in the care of its wearer, because too much grooming reduces the curls. This slightly unkempt appearance is part of the cat's appeal.

Their character is similar to that of their outcross breeds. Although they can be playful and inquisitive, these are easygoing cats, never in a hurry, and content to be near their owners.

worst Devon with a Chartreux body." Newman decided that a shorter, more rounded head, and slightly longer coat (to show off that curl) would be ideal, and so bred Pest to her own Persian.

The resultant litter contained three curly-coated and three straight-coated kittens, confirming the gene to be a dominant. One of these kittens was bred to Persians, Exotics, and British Shorthairs, all of which are still allowed as outcross breeds. He was also bred back to Pest. No serious problems connected with the gene came to light. The breedings also established that the gene was a simple dominant, eliminating the possibility that it was the same trait as the American Wirehair. Newman

named the breed after her father's family name and the Selkirk Mountains, and began to show the cats, finding instant popularity. The

Early signs

Curly-coated Selkirk Rexes can be distinguished from their straight-coated littermates at birth by their curly whiskers. These are brittle, and the ends may break off as they grow. Sometimes, rexed coats change as kittens grow up, but this is not true of the Selkirk: If they are curly at birth, they will remain curly as an adult, although the adult coat may show less curl.

American Wirehair

ORIGIN United States (1960s)

SYNONYM None

WEIGHT 8–15 lb. (3.5–7 kg.)

BUILD 🐈

TEMPERAMENT 🐈

COAT CARE 🪮

COLORS Western colors in self, tortie, bicolor, smoke, shaded, and tipped; blotched and striped tabby patterns

As North America's first home-grown rexed cat, the Wirehair certainly did not win in the naming stakes. Such an unstrokable name may have helped hold the breed back from greater success, although today slightly painful puns about "getting wired" are in play in an attempt to improve its fortunes with a new generation.

BLACK SELF

WHITE

CREAM STRIPED TABBY

BLUE SILVER TABBY

SILVER SHADED

TORTIE TABBY & WHITE

BREED ORIGINS

The first Wirehair was a red and white male, the only survivor in a litter of free breeding barn cats in Verona, New York. The year was 1966, so the Cornish Rex was already a Championship breed, raising the profile of unusual coats. The male, Council Rock Farm Adam, was bred to a straight-coated female, and the resulting kinked coats showed the mutation to be dominant.

Wirehairs were first accepted for CFA registration in 1967 and for Championship competition in 1978, and are also recognized by other North American associations including TICA. However, only a few tens of cats are registered each year, and they are rarer abroad.

OWNING A WIREHAIR

The breed was developed using the American Shorthair as an outcross breed. As a result, the standard of the Wirehair is similar to that of the American Shorthair in type, the crimped coat being the principal distinguishing feature. This has moved away from the founding father's wedge-shaped head, large ears, and slanted eyes. The coat is generally coarse and springy. This rexing trait is an "incomplete dominant," so cats may be anything from slightly wavy to tightly crimped, and litters usually contain at least one straight-coated kitten, making progress all the more difficult. The coat is rather unstable, with the hardest types breaking easily, and cats sometimes shed almost all their hair due to relatively minor stress, such as a change in the weather. Longhairs do appear from time to time, but are not shown: They are said to look like "dust bunnies."

If you are lucky, the coat is low maintenance, and best without grooming. Wirehairs can be prone to skin allergies and heavy production of earwax, however, so regular cleaning and bathing without brushing may be necessary, although this is no more onerous than the grooming needs of several longer-haired breeds. Other than this, the breed is generally hardy and healthy.

In personality, Wirehairs are close to their Shorthair outcross: Playful and friendly, but generally quiet and laidback individuals.

BROWN TABBY Tabbies and bicolors predominate, but the haywire crimping of the coat produces some strange effects on tabby patterns, sometimes making identification hard.

LaPerm

ORIGIN United States (1980s)
SYNONYM Dalles LaPerm
WEIGHT 8–12 lb. (3.5–5.5 kg.)
BUILD
TEMPERAMENT
COAT CARE
COLORS All colors in all shades and all patterns

Despite the quirky name, this breed is not the result of any human hairdressing or other tinkering, but a mutation that turned up in free-breeding rural American cats. Although it has not yet climbed the popularity tables in its homeland, it has become established overseas in Europe and as far afield as New Zealand.

BLACK SELF   WHITE   RED SELF   CREAM STRIPED TABBY   BLUE TORTIE TABBY & WHITE   SEAL TABBY POINT

BREED ORIGINS

The first LaPerm appeared in a litter of kittens born to a working barn cat: She was bald, with a "blueprint" of a tabby pattern on her skin, and within eight weeks she began to grow a coat, but one that was soft and full of curls. Her owners, the Koehls, named her Curly, and she bred to local toms. Further controlled breeding confirmed that the mutant gene was dominant. Eventually the cats were entered in a show and generated enormous interest. The breed is recognized by CFA and has full Championship status within TICA. GCCF registries for the breed opened in 2004, but it is not yet recognized by FIFé.

OWNING A LAPERM

The LaPerm coat is fairly soft, comes in long and short versions, and varies in curl from waves to ringlets. Kittens may be born hairless, curly, or straight-coated, and often lose any hair at about two weeks, regrowing it over the next months. The build is slender.

Springing from a large pool of free-breeding cats, the LaPerm is generally healthy. As might be expected from their barn cat beginnings, they are also intelligent, inquisitive, and active, but they are more gregarious and people-oriented than their forebears.

BLUE TICKED TABBY The texture of the shorthair coat is generally firmer and springier than the longhaired variety. The coat is light and airy, standing away from the body.

Sphynx

ORIGIN North America and Europe (1970s)
SYNONYM Canadian Hairless
WEIGHT 8–15 lb. (3.5–7 kg.)
BUILD 🐈
TEMPERAMENT 🐈
COAT CARE ✂️
COLORS All colors in all shades and all patterns

Few breeds will divide those who see them into "love them" and "hate them" camps so starkly as the Sphynx. Although they are bred and shown in all major world registries, public opinion is more divided. To their fans, Sphynxes are amazing, even magical; to others they can seem unnatural, even monstrous.

LILAC SELF   BLACK & WHITE   BLUE TORTIE & WHITE   SEAL POINT   BLUE POINT

BREED ORIGINS

In 1966, a shorthaired domestic cat gave birth to a hairless kitten in Toronto, Canada. Aptly named Prune, he was mated to his mother and began the first hairless breeding program.

CFA withdrew support for the breeding program in 1971, believing the gene to carry lethal problems. It is hard to be certain whether the modern Sphynx is descended from Prune or from other hairless cats that appeared, apparently having the same mutation, and were taken into the

BLACK AND WHITE The Sphynx is medium sized and medium boned with a well-developed musculature. The torso and belly are rounded.

breeding program. A breeding pair from Prune was sent to Dr. Hugo Hernandez in the Netherlands, and in the late 1970s, he was sent two more females from a litter in Toronto. He bred the queens to a Devon Rex to keep the line going.

From this foundation, the breed spread to France, the United Kingdom,

BLUE AND WHITE Although the head looks angular and Oriental, the build of the Sphynx is not delicate. If anything, it is sometimes reminiscent of a bulldog.

and back over the Atlantic to the United States. Here, two more hairless females were acquired by Oregon breeder Kim Mueske in 1981, bred to Devon Rexes, and included in the Sphynx program.

TICA and FIFé recognized the Sphynx in the 1990s; in 1999 it was accepted in Australia. CFA only gave Championship status in 2002, and the GCCF began registering Sphynxes in 2006, but does not intend to register "any other hair-deficient breeds."

OWNING A SPHYNX

The Sphynx is not truly hairless, but retains a covering of peachlike down,

LILAC AND WHITE Colors are shown in blueprint form on the skin. Exact colors can be hard to determine; FIFé, which has codes for colors, has adopted a new set for hairless cats.

sometimes a little more on the tail tip, bridge of nose, and ears. They are warm to the touch—they have been described as suede-covered hot-water bottles.

Oils that would normally disperse along the hair shafts accumulate on the skin in hairless breeds, so regular bathing is a must. Injury is more likely with no cushioning coat, and for this reason, coupled with the sensitivity to cold in winter and potential for sunburn in summer, most experts feel these cats to be indoor only animals. The lack of insulation also means the Sphynx burns more calories than feeding guidelines predict for a cat of its size.

If it lives in a suitable environment, the Sphynx has a reputation as being loving and playful, always ready to act the clown, and keen to curl up with its owner for warmth.

TABBY POINT Cats with white or pale skin are the most vulnerable to sunburn. If cats are allowed outside, sunscreen on areas such as the tips of the ears may be advisable.

Manx

ORIGIN Isle of Man (before 1700s)

SYNONYM None

WEIGHT 8–12 lb. (3.5–5.5 kg.)

BUILD 🐈

TEMPERAMENT 🐈

COAT CARE 🪥

COLORS All colors in self, tortie, bicolor, solid, smoke, and tipped; blotched, striped, and spotted tabby patterns; pointed pattern in TICA only

If this famous symbol of the Isle of Man were to appear for the first time today, it would be unlikely to win such wide acceptance. This is a curious breed whose movements were described by one early breeder as "a comical sight calculated to excite laughter in the most mournfully disposed person."

| BLACK SELF | BLUE SELF | BLUE & WHITE | BROWN CLASSIC TABBY | RED STRIPED TABBY | TORTIE |

BLACK SELF This cat could not be shown in most associations, which demand a smooth rump, with no stub of bone large enough to feel. However, "stumpies" with tails up to 1¼ in. (3 cm.) can win awards in FIFé.

BREED ORIGINS

The rarity or absence of the Manx mutation across the rest of Europe, and indeed the world, may mean that it is a local occurrence, or that due to its health implications, the mutation survived only in the limited breeding population of an island. Manx cats were shown from the start of the United Kingdom cat fancy in the 19th century. They were accepted by registries abroad quite early, with CFA accepting them in 1920. Pointed Manx have been developed, initially in Australia, but are accepted only in TICA; the longhaired Cymric is more widely recognized.

BROWN TABBY AND WHITE Although fairly popular in the United States, where it falls about halfway down the ranking by number, the Manx is increasingly rare in its homeland.

OWNING A MANX

The Manx gene is an incomplete dominant, with varying effect. Cats may be longies (with a long, although not full-length tail), stumpies (with a short stub of a tail), and rumpies (with no tail). The gene, sadly, is semilethal or sublethal: Homozygous kittens, with two copies of the gene, are stillborn, or die early in development and are reabsorbed. Surviving cats occasionally have fused vertebrae and pelvic bones. The spinal cord may be shorter than normal, leaving the cat with poor control of its bowel, bladder, and hind legs. Because of these problems, it is vital to obtain kittens from a responsible breeder.

These large cats can be surprisingly quiet. They are affectionate, and have been described as doglike, padding around after their owners.

Cymric

ORIGIN Canada and United States (1960s)

SYNONYM Longhaired Manx

WEIGHT 8–12 lb. (3.5–5.5 kg.)

BUILD 🐈

TEMPERAMENT 🐈

COAT CARE ✐

COLORS All colors in self, tortie, bicolor, solid, smoke, and tipped; blotched, striped, and spotted tabby patterns; pointed pattern

The name of this breed comes from Cymru, the Welsh name for Wales. Welsh spelling and pronunciation are quirky: Cymru is pronounced (approximately) *Koomree*, with the first syllable stressed, and Cymric is pronounced *Koomrick*, although *Kimrick* is common. But there is actually nothing Welsh about this breed.

RED SELF

BLACK & WHITE

RED & WHITE

BROWN STRIPED TABBY

TORTIE

BLUE TORTIE & WHITE

COPPER EYED WHITE The short body of the breed is in part another effect of the gene for taillessness. This can affect the vertebrae all the way up the spine, making them shorter than usual.

OWNING A CYMRIC

The first task if you want to own a Cymric is to find one. Cymrics are by no means common, although they are seen more frequently in North America than elsewhere. Cymrics are essentially higher-maintenance Manx that need grooming two or three times a week. The same cautions about health apply, and they have the same peaceable nature.

BREED ORIGINS

Because this breed is simply a longhaired Manx, it largely shares the same origins. The longhair trait may have been brought into the Isle of Man's busy ports by ships' cats.

The Cymric was first shown in North America in the 1960s. The name was chosen by Blair Wright and Leslie Falteisek, breeders from Canada and the United States respectively, as Wright's grandmother said that she had seen longhaired, tailless cats in Wales. The Cymric was recognized by the Canadian Cat Association in the 1970s. TICA and CFA both followed by the end of the 1980s, and FIFé finally accepted the breed in 2006. The GCCF is very unlikely ever to recognize it: Its policies now rule against potentially harmful traits. In 1994, CFA dropped the name Cymric and revised the Manx standard to include both longhair and shorthair divisions. In other associations, longhaired Manx are automatically classed as Cymric.

CREAM SELF The coat is moderately long over most of the body, and noticeably longer on the ruff, the abdomen, and the fluffy britches on the hind legs.

Japanese Bobtail

ORIGIN Japan (before 1800s)

SYNONYM None

WEIGHT 6–9 lb. (2.5–4 kg.)

BUILD 🐈

TEMPERAMENT 🐈

COAT CARE 🖌

COLORS All colors in self, tortie and bicolor; striped, blotched, and spotted tabby patterns

This short-tailed, endearing breed was something of a Japanese cultural ambassador to the United States after World War II. Although still far behind the Thai-derived breeds in popularity, Japan's traditional good luck cat has a secure place in the hearts of the American and European cat fancy.

 BLACK SELF

 RED SELF

 BLACK & WHITE

BROWN STRIPED TABBY

 TORTIE & WHITE

 BLUE TORTIE & WHITE

BREED ORIGINS

The early history of bobtailed cats is not known. There is a tradition that cats were brought to Japan in 999AD, but in fact they arrived centuries before this. In the classic *Tale of Genji*, thought to have been completed by 1021, a character obtains a Chinese cat, which is distinguished from the "swarms" of Japanese cats and said to be more affectionate; bobbed tails are not mentioned.

Cats with shortened, kinked, and pompom tails are found throughout southeast Asia, but they are more

RED TABBY AND WHITE
The first kittens imported to the United States included a red and white male. CFA still allows only traditional Western colors.

numerous on the Japanese islands. This could be because a high proportion of the first cats to arrive were bobtailed, or because they were particularly favored by the Japanese.

Cats were not pampered court pets in Japan—indeed for a time they were

RED TABBY AND WHITE This breeding male has developed the typical stud jowls and a rather sturdy build; the breed standards are more favorable to female cats.

Tales of tails

The Japanese Bobtail has acquired a legend or two. The most popular is that once a cat warming itself by the fire crept too close and set its tail alight. In a panic, it raced from the house and through the streets, in the process setting fire to houses throughout the city. As a punishment, and so that such a thing could not happen again, the emperor decreed that all cats should have their tails cut short. On a happier note, the Bobtail is said to be the original Maneki Neko, a Japanese lucky mascot.

These cats may have become popular in Japan because of another legend. It was believed that a cat could become a *bakeneko*, a monster with shapeshifting abilities and the power of speech, if it reached a certain age or size or if its tail became forked: A cat with a short tail might seem to carry less risk.

apparently an incomplete dominant. But they were not really prized until after World War II, when American service personnel brought cats home to the United States with them. Breeders Elizabeth Freret and Lynn Beck imported kittens and wrote a standard. This emphasized a more slender cat than the cobby types often seen in Japan, insuring it was distinct from the chunky Manx, the only other tailless breed of the time. The Bobtail is now recognized by every major registry except the GCCF. The shorthair, sleek but not as flat coated as some other Oriental breeds, was the first recognized but carried the longhair gene within it. Only the shorthair is recognized by FIFé.

OWNING A BOBTAIL

Both the longhair and shorthair coats are silky and easycare, unless the cat needs bathing, at which time they prove quite water repellent. Japanese Bobtails are a healthy breed: The mutation that causes the shortened tail does not seem to have any other effects.

They are intelligent and lively cats with a reputation for enjoying carrying things in their mouths and playing fetch, like dogs, and being less averse to a dip than many breeds. Sociable and talkative, but with soft voices, they are recommended for multicat homes, especially if their owners are not going to be around much.

forbidden as pets, because all were needed to protect everything from scrolls and silk worms to rice stores from vermin. Bobtails are found in Japanese art from courtesans' portraits to scenes from rural life. They appear not as a separate breed, but in mixed groups of cats, in all coats, although predominantly a van pattern of white with just a few areas of color.

Bobtails were remarked on by curious Westerners for centuries, and suggested as a possible source of the Manx. This theory is now discounted, because this is a separate mutation, although also

TORTIE AND WHITE Called *mi-ke* in this breed, this is a prized combination, especially with the addition of odd-colored eyes. The spots may be of mixed colors or separate.

Scottish Fold

ORIGIN Scotland (1960s)
SYNONYM None
WEIGHT 6–13 lb. (2.5–6 kg.)
BUILD 🐈
TEMPERAMENT 🐈
COAT CARE 🖌 🖌
COLORS Western colors in self, tortie, bicolor, smoke, shaded, and tipped; all tabby patterns; pointed pattern in TICA

Originally called "lops" because their ears resembled those of lop-eared rabbits, these cats have also been likened to owls or teddy bears. They are certainly unmistakable. Although Scottish in origin, they are now an American breed: European registries are reluctant to recognize breeds with such abnormalities.

BLUE SELF   RED SELF   BROWN CLASSIC TABBY   SILVER STRIPED TABBY   TORTIE   BLUE TORTIE & WHITE

BREED ORIGINS

Scottish Folds trace their parentage back to Susie, a barn cat from Tayside in Scotland. When her grandson was bred to a white British Shorthair, the resulting litter contained five folded-ear kittens. The GCCF initially accepted the breed in 1966, but then suspended registration by 1971 due to concerns that the folded ears could give rise to ear-mite infestation or hearing problems. The breeding program crossed the Atlantic, and breeders began to work for CFA recognition, which they achieved by 1978. The breed is also recognized by TICA, but not by FIFé or the GCCF.

From the start, many Folds had shortened, stiffened tails, and in the 1970s, x-rays of cats showed skeletal problems. The Fold gene affects cartilage beyond the ears, and all cats with the gene suffer from progressive arthritis of varying degrees of severity. For this reason, cats with folded ears are always bred to straight-eared cats, and outcrossing to the British Shorthair and American Shorthair continues.

OWNING A FOLD

It is vital to buy a Fold only from a reputable breeder following a careful and responsible breeding program. The length and the flexibility of the tail are important as an early indicator of problems, but joint problems may appear as the cat matures and ages. In character, this is a gentle, calm cat.

BLUE-CREAM AND WHITE
The earliest Scottish Folds included longhairs. However, the breeders pressed for recognition of shorthairs first, and longhairs had to wait far longer for their turn.

American Curl

ORIGIN United States (1980s)

SYNONYM None

WEIGHT 7–11 lb. (3–5 kg.)

BUILD 🐈

TEMPERAMENT 🐱

COAT CARE 🖌

COLORS All colors in all shades and all patterns

The cat fancy is often fanciful, but something about the sweet, slightly quizzical look of the Curl spurs breeders to new heights. The founders are happy to embrace the tag of "designer" cats for their breed, describing them as "signed masterpieces of a humor-loving Creator." It seems every aspect of the Curl provokes a smile.

| BLACK SELF | BLUE SILVER TABBY | TORTIE | RED STRIPED TABBY & WHITE | BROWN TABBY & WHITE | LILAC TABBY POINT |

BREED ORIGINS

The foundation female of the breed was a longhaired black stray, named Shulamith, with strangely curled ears, who passed on the trait to her kittens. Curls were first shown in 1983, and the unusual mutation was established to be a simple dominant. The breed had Championship status in TICA by 1987 and CFA by 1993. It is not recognized by FIFé or the GCCF, whose registration policies exclude any new breeds with skeletal or cartilage abnormalities.

OWNING A CURL

The ears are straight when the kitten is born, but usually within a week they have begun to curl. The breed standard is based on the look of Shulamith, and the only outcrossing allowed is to nonpedigree domestic cats that closely match the breed standard. Curls are healthy and robust, with no breed-specific problems. Both the shorthair and the semilonghair coats are silky and sleek, requiring little attention. These are lively, busy cats that are fond of play.

RED TABBY AND WHITE Ears can curl a little or a lot. The ears of show-quality cats must curl through a full crescent, with the tips pointing down at the skull.

Munchkin

ORIGIN United States (1980s)

SYNONYM None

WEIGHT 5–9 lb. (2.5–4 kg.)

BUILD

TEMPERAMENT

COAT CARE

COLORS All colors in all shades and all patterns

This breed has the legs that launched a thousand flame wars in breeder forums. Although some objections have been born of genuine concern for its welfare, others have been sheer gut reaction to its physique. Whichever side you take on this divisive issue, short-legged cats seem to be here to stay.

BLACK SELF   RED & WHITE   BROWN STRIPED TABBY   TORTIE TABBY & WHITE   BLUE TABBY & WHITE   SEAL POINT

BREED ORIGINS

Dwarfed cats were reported in the United Kingdom in the 1930s and 1940s, Russia in the 1950s, and New England in the 1970s. In 1983, Sandra Hochenedel adopted a short-legged, pregnant black cat she found living under a trailer in Louisiana, and named her Blackberry. Half the kittens were short legged, and one of them, a male named Toulouse, was given to Kay LaFrance, who established a free-breeding colony of Munchkins, named after the race from *The Wizard of Oz*, on her plantation.

As awareness of the Munchkin grew, many other cats with this dominant mutation were found, and some were registered and added to the breeding stock. TICA gave the Munchkin Championship status in 2002, not without internal strife. It has been recognized in Australia, but CFA does not recognize it and both the GCCF and FIFé have stated their policies would not allow a new breed based on such a trait. In recent years there have been several proposed "spin-off" breeds from the Munchkin, generally with cute names, such as hairless Minskins, curl-eared Kinkalows, and rexed Skookums. The last was recognized in Australia and as an Experimental breed by TICA in 2006.

TORTOISESHELL AND WHITE The Munchkin is recognized in both shorthair and longhair versions. The long coat should be flowing and silky, with shaggy britches and a plumed tail.

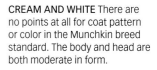

CREAM AND WHITE There are no points at all for coat pattern or color in the Munchkin breed standard. The body and head are both moderate in form.

From the start, Munchkins aroused strong feelings. To their fans, they are as valid as breeds with curly hair, no hair, short tails, no tails, folded ears, or curled ears. To others, their reduced stature is a quirk too far. Where free-ranging pet cats are usual, they look cruelly vulnerable, although short-legged feral families have been recorded surviving for several generations.

There has been concern about health issues, although spinal problems caused by too much flexing of a long spine carried on short legs have not materialized. Some suffer a skeletal abnormality called thoracic lordosis, but this is also found in long-legged breeds.

There are possible problems inherent in the mutation: When two short-legged cats are bred together, litters are often small, so the gene may be lethal when two copies are carried. However, it does not seem to cause other problems, unlike the skeletal abnormalities of the Manx or Scottish Fold.

OWNING A MUNCHKIN

North America and Australia have most of the Munchkins and derivative breeds; elsewhere, they are likely to be hard to find. They can and do run, climb, and even jump, although onto chairs rather than wardrobes. An indoor life may be safest, but these cats still have a full size need for activity and entertainment.

LILAC SELF The dwarfism in the Munchkin can cause the legs to be not only short but also slightly bowed.

Bengal

ORIGIN United States (1980s)

SYNONYM Once called Leopardettes

WEIGHT 12–22 lb. (5.5–10 kg.)

BUILD 🐈

TEMPERAMENT 🐆

COAT CARE 🖌

COLORS Brown blotched and spotted tabby, or with pointed pattern over tabby

The standard bearer for all the hybrid breeds, the Bengal has taken a long time to gain acceptance in mainstream registries and still causes some controversy. Whatever its critics say, this is a tremendously popular breed: Since recognition in the United Kingdom, for example, it has soared to third place in terms of numbers, overtaking several old favorites on the way.

SNOW BENGAL Sepia, mink, and pointed patterns all appear. Snows should have an ivory to cream base coat and a "pearl dusting."

BREED ORIGINS

In the 1960s, there was an accidental mating between an Asian leopard cat and a black, shorthaired domestic cat at the home of breeder Jean Sugden in California. In the early 1970s, now remarried and called Jean Mill, she received several more such hybrids, which had been bred as part of a research project into feline leukaemia immunity. The hybrids were used to form the basis of an entirely new breed, the first intentional hybrid of a wild and a domestic cat to seek recognition. The name was taken from the scientific name for the leopard cat, *Prionailurus bengalensis*.

To develop the spotted coat, breeders soon turned to using street cats from India, chosen for their coat patterns, and Egyptian Maus. The breeders' aim was to replicate the look of the wild ancestry, while breeding towards a tractable domestic pet.

The developing Bengal breed was presented to CFA in the 1970s, seeking recognition, but the cats presented were foundation cats, within three generations of original crosses to the wild cat, and not really domestic. CFA still does not recognize the Bengal. TICA began registering more developed cats in 1983, and finally granted them Championship status in 1991. The GCCF and FIFé followed suit in Europe, together with registries in Australia and New Zealand, throughout the 1990s. As a rule, recognition has come with the stipulation that crossing back to the wild species had to stop, and only cats from the fourth generation down from an original cross are allowed in studbooks.

BROWN SPOTTED This was the first Bengal pattern and the first to be recognized by most associations. The spots may vary in size and shape, but large markings are preferred.

OWNING A BENGAL

Bengals are relatively large, and substantial in appearance. Originally there was just a spotted coat, but new variations have appeared and the status of these varies from one association to another. There are the "snow" colors, the result of the recessive pointed gene. Marbled cats, with a modified blotched tabby pattern, are also accepted. More recently silver Bengals with a white undercoat have appeared. These are so far accepted in only a few associations.

Anecdotally, Bengals seem to have a greater incidence than other breeds of irritable bowel syndrome (IBS). The cereal content in commercial cat foods seems a particular irritant, and finding an appropriate food may take time. Bengals may also be vulnerable to microscopic parasites that cause bowel problems; owners in areas without chlorinated water supplies may want to take the precaution of only giving water that has been boiled.

Breeders are adamant that Bengals are people oriented and mix well with other pets and children. They do stress, however, that they can be mischievous, boisterous, and active.

SEAL SEPIA SPOTTED The Bengal coat often has a glitter effect. It is caused by transparent areas at the hair tip (called mica) or along the shaft (called satin).

INDEX